D0152384

Bloom's BioCritiques

Bloom's BioCritiques

T.S. ELIOT

Edited and with an introduction by
Harold Bloom
Sterling Professor of the Humanities
Yale University

CHELSEA HOUSE
PUBLISHERS
A Haights Cross Communications Company

Philadelphia

A Haights Cross Communications ⟁ Company

Library of Congress Cataloging-in-Publication Data

T.S. Eliot / edited and with an introduction by Harold Bloom.
        p. cm. -- (Bloom's Biocritiques)
"Works by T.S. Eliot": p.
Includes bibliographical references (p.) and index.
    ISBN 0-7910-7384-X
    1. Eliot, T.S. (Thomas Stearns), 1888–1965--Criticism and
interpretation. I. Bloom, Harold. II. Series.
    PS3509.L43Z87243 2003
    821'.912--dc21

                                                    2003006756

Chelsea House Publishers
1974 Sproul Road, Suite 400
Broomall, PA 19008-0914

http://www.chelseahouse.com

Contributing editor: Portia Williams Weiskel

Cover design by Keith Trego

Cover: © Hulton/Archive by Getty Images.

Layout by EJB Publishing Services

CONTENTS

USER'S GUIDE

These volumes are designed to introduce the reader to the life and work of the world's literary masters. Each volume begins with Harold Bloom's essay "The Work in the Writer" and a volume-specific introduction also written by Professor Bloom. Following these unique introductions is an engaging biography that discusses the major life events and important literary accomplishments of the author under consideration.

Furthermore, each volume includes an original critique that not only traces the themes, symbols, and ideas apparent in the author's works, but strives to put those works into a cultural and historical perspective. In addition to the original critique is a brief selection of significant critical essays previously published on the author and his or her works followed by a concise and informative chronology of the writer's life. Finally, each volume concludes with a bibliography of the writer's works, a list of additional readings, and an index of important themes and ideas.

HAROLD BLOOM

The Work in the Writer

Literary biography found its masterpiece in James Boswell's *Life of Samuel Johnson*. Boswell, when he treated Johnson's writings, implicitly commented upon Johnson as found in his work, even as in the great critic's life. Modern instances of literary biography, such as Richard Ellmann's lives of W. B. Yeats, James Joyce, and Oscar Wilde, essentially follow in Boswell's pattern.

That the writer somehow is in the work, we need not doubt, though with William Shakespeare, writer-of-writers, we almost always need to rely upon pure surmise. The exquisite rancidities of the Problem Plays or Dark Comedies seem to express an extraordinary estrangement of Shakespeare from himself. When we read or attend *Troilus and Cressida* and *Measure for Measure*, we may be startled by particular speeches of Ulysses in the first play, or of Vincentio in the second. These speeches, of Ulysses upon hierarchy or upon time, or of Duke Vincentio upon death, are too strong either for their contexts or for the characters of their speakers. The same phenomenon occurs with Parolles, the military impostor of *All's Well That Ends Well*. Utterly disgraced, he nevertheless affirms: "Simply the thing I am/Shall make me live."

In Shakespeare, more even than in his peers, Dante and Cervantes, meaning always starts itself again through excess or overflow. The strongest of Shakespeare's creatures—Falstaff, Hamlet, Iago, Lear, Cleopatra—have an exuberance that is fiercer than their plays can contain. If Ben Jonson was at all correct in his complaint that "Shakespeare wanted art," it could have been only in a sense that he may not have intended. Where do the personalities of Falstaff or Hamlet touch a limit? What was it in Shakespeare that made the two parts of *Henry IV* and *Hamlet* into "plays unlimited"? Neither Falstaff nor Hamlet will be stopped: their wit, their beautiful, laughing speech, their intensity of being—all these are virtually infinite.

In what ways do Falstaff and Hamlet manifest the writer in the work? Evidently, we can never know, or know enough to answer with any authority. But what would happen if we reversed the question, and asked: How did the work form the writer, Shakespeare?

Of Shakespeare's inwardness, his biography tells us nothing. And yet, to an astonishing extent, Shakespeare created our inwardness. At the least, we can speculate that Shakespeare so lived his life as to conceal the depths of his nature, particularly as he rather prematurely aged. We do not have Shakespeare on Shakespeare, as any good reader of the Sonnets comes to realize: they do not constitute a key that unlocks his heart. No sequence of sonnets could be less confessional or more powerfully detached from the poet's self.

The German poet and universal genius, Goethe, affords a superb contrast to Shakespeare. Of Goethe's life, we know more than everything; I wonder sometimes if we know as much about Napoleon or Freud or any other human being who ever has lived, as we know about Goethe. Everywhere, we can find Goethe in his work, so much so that Goethe seems to crowd the writing out, just as Byron and Oscar Wilde seem to usurp their own literary accomplishments. Goethe, cunning beyond measure, nevertheless invested a rival exuberance in his greatest works that could match his personal charisma. The sublime outrageousness of the Second Part of *Faust*, or of the greater lyric and meditative poems, form a Counter-Sublime to Goethe's own daemonic intensity.

Goethe was fascinated by the daemonic in himself; we can doubt that Shakespeare had any such interests. Evidently, Shakespeare abandoned his acting career just before he composed *Measure for Measure* and *Othello*. I surmise that the egregious interventions by Vincentio and Iago displace the actor's energies into a new kind of mischief-making, a fresh opening to a subtler playwriting-within-the-play.

But what had opened Shakespeare to this new awareness? The answer is the work in the writer, *Hamlet* in Shakespeare. One can go further: it was not so much the play, *Hamlet*, as the character Hamlet, who changed Shakespeare's art forever.

Hamlet's personality is so large and varied that it rivals Goethe's own. Ironically Goethe's Faust, his Hamlet, has no personality at all, and is as colorless as Shakespeare himself seems to have chosen to be. Yet nothing could be more colorful than the Second Part of *Faust*, which is peopled by an astonishing array of monsters, grotesque devils, and classical ghosts.

A contrast between Shakespeare and Goethe demonstrates that in each—but in very different ways—we can better find the work in the person, than we can discover that banal entity, the person in the work. Goethe to many of his contemporaries, seemed to be a mortal god. Shakespeare, so far as we know, seemed an affable, rather ordinary fellow, who aged early and became somewhat withdrawn. Yet Faust, though Mephistopheles battles for his soul, is hardly worth the trouble unless you take him as an idea and not as a person. Hamlet is nearly every-idea-in-one, but he is precisely a personality and a person.

Would Hamlet be so astonishingly persuasive if his father's ghost did not haunt him? Falstaff is more alive than Prince Hal, who says that the devil haunts him in the shape of an old fat man. Three years before composing the final *Hamlet*, Shakespeare invented Falstaff, who then never ceased to haunt his creator. Falstaff and Hamlet may be said to best represent the work in the writer, because their influence upon Shakespeare was prodigious. W.H. Auden accurately observed that Falstaff possesses infinite energy: never tired, never bored, and absolutely both witty and happy until Hal's rejection destroys him. Hamlet too has infinite energy, but in him it is more curse than blessing.

Falstaff and Hamlet can be said to occupy the roles in Shakespeare's invented world that Sancho Panza and Don Quixote possess in Cervantes's. Shakespeare's plays from 1610 on (starting with *Twelfth Night*) are thus analogous to the Second Part of Cervantes's epic novel. Sancho and the Don overtly jostle Cervantes for authorship in the Second Part, even as Cervantes battles against the impostor who has pirated a continuation of his work. As a dramatist, Shakespeare manifests the work in the writer more indirectly. Falstaff's prose genius is revived in the scapegoating of Malvolio by Maria and Sir Toby Belch, while Falstaff's darker insights are developed by Feste's melancholic wit. Hamlet's intellectual resourcefulness, already deadly, becomes poisonous in Iago and in Edmund. Yet we have not crossed into the deeper abysses of the work in the writer in later Shakespeare.

No fictive character, before or since, is Falstaff's equal in self-trust. Sir John, whose delight in himself is contagious, has total confidence both in his self-awareness and in the resources of his language. Hamlet, whose self is as strong, and whose language is as copious, nevertheless distrusts both the self and language. Later Shakespeare is, as it were, much under the influence both of Falstaff and of Hamlet, but they tug him in opposite directions. Shakespeare's own copiousness of language is well-nigh incredible: a vocabulary in excess of twenty-one thousand words, almost eighteen hundred of which he coined himself. And of his word-hoard, nearly half are used only once each, as though the perfect setting for each had been found, and need not be repeated. Love for language and faith in language are Falstaffian attributes. Hamlet will darken both that love and that faith in Shakespeare, and perhaps the Sonnets can best be read as Falstaff and Hamlet counterpointing against one another.

Can we surmise how aware Shakespeare was of Falstaff and Hamlet, once they had played themselves into existence? *Henry IV, Part I* appeared in six quarto editions during Shakespeare's lifetime; *Hamlet* possibly had four. Falstaff and Hamlet were played again and again at the Globe, but Shakespeare knew also that they were being read, and he must have had contact with some of those readers. What would it have been like to discuss Falstaff or Hamlet with one of their early readers (presumably also part of their audience at the Globe), if you were the creator of such demiurges? The question would seem nonsensical to most Shakespeare scholars, but then these days they tend to be either ideologues or moldy figs. How can we recover the uncanniness of Falstaff and of Hamlet, when they now have become so familiar?

A writer's influence upon himself is an unexplored problem in criticism, but such an influence is never free from anxieties. The biocritical problem (which this series attempts to explore) can be divided into two areas, difficult to disengage fully. Accomplished works affect the author's life, and also affect her subsequent writings. It is simpler for me to surmise the effect of *Mrs. Dalloway* and *To the Lighthouse* upon Woolf's late *Between the Acts*, than it is to relate Clarissa Dalloway's suicide and Lily Briscoe's capable endurance in art to the tragic death and complex life of Virginia Woolf.

There are writers whose lives were so vivid that they seem sometimes to obscure the literary achievement: Byron, Wilde, Malraux, Hemingway. But most major Western writers do not live that exuberantly, and the greatest of all, Shakespeare, sometimes appears to have adopted the personal mask of colorlessness. And yet there are heroes of literature who struggled titanically with their own eras—Tolstoy, Milton, Victor Hugo—who nevertheless matter more for their works than their lives.

There are great figures—Emily Dickinson, Wallace Stevens, Willa Cather—who seem to have had so little of the full intensity of life when compared to the vitality of their work, that we might almost speak of the work in the work, rather than even of the work in a person. Emily Brontë might well be the extreme instance of such a visionary, surpassing William Blake in that one regard.

I conclude this general introduction to a series of literary bio-critiques by stating a tentative formula or principle for gauging the many ways in which the work influences the person and her subsequent, later work. Our influence upon ourselves is always related to the Shakespearean invention of self-overhearing, which I have written about in several other contexts. Life, as well as poetry and prose, is overheard rather than simply heard. The writer listens to herself as though she were somebody else, and the will to change begins to operate. The forces that live in us include the prior work we have done, and the dreams and waking visions that evade our dismissals.

HAROLD BLOOM

Introduction

These days, turning celebrated writers out of their closets is an academic blood-sport. Homoeroticism is the usual revelation: Henry James, D.H. Lawrence, Thomas Mann, Balzac, and T.S. Eliot are among the many titans who have been outed. But the putative list is legion: most feminist critics have welcomed Emily Dickinson to Lesbian culture, there supposedly to join Virginia Woolf, H.D., Elizabeth Bishop, May Swenson, Marianne Moore, and Willa Cather, among many others.

I see no end to this critical fashion: perhaps the real objection to the Dead White European Males is their overwhelming heterosexuality. For every Proust, there are five Flauberts. In the delighted rush to expose, distinctions tend to vanish. Certainly, the elderly Henry James wrote love letters to literary young men, and put on makeup to have high tea with Rupert Brooke. But there is little to suggest that the master actually engaged in sex, while D.H. Lawrence, despite an occasional wrestling-match with John Middleton Murry, achieved ecstasy by anal intercourse with his wife, Frieda. Balzac cultivated promising young men, as did his heroically wicked Vautrin, but Balzac's actual sexual activities were perfectly traditional, though never on the grand scale of Victor Hugo's.

T.S. Eliot in this, as in all things, is nuanced and evasive. There may have been a homoerotic relation with Jean Verdenal, but we don't know. Eliot had a ghastly first marriage, evidently unconsummated, and much later, a happy second marriage. His most characteristic poetry, composed during his great decade of 1915–1925, generally visualizes heterosexuality as a blight akin to urban decay, cultural decline, and the Jews, always his favorite black beasts.

I have no idea what Eliot, a British subject, would have done had Hitler successfully invaded and occupied Britain. Though he was too proper to join the English Fascists, it seems quite accurate to characterize him as a French Fascist, deeply influenced by the Action Française of Charles Maurras, which ascribed France's decline to the influence of women and Jews.

Christopher Ricks, a formidable scholar, has labored to cleanse Eliot of anti-Semitism, but Eliot's poetry and prose delightedly exult in it, though rarely with the vulgarity of his close friends, Ezra Pound and Wyndham Lewis. In Eliot, the anti-Semitism is simply a mark of the authenticity of his Neo-Christianity.

I myself, aside from being both Jewish and a Romantic critic of literature, never have been able to tolerate Eliot's prose, whether critical, cultural, or devotional. The poetry, down to 1925, is another matter: impossible to love, impossible to forget. The Eliot of the "Preludes" and *The Waste Land* is a permanent poet, whether one loathes him or not. He is hardly the only abominable human being to have written great poetry.

It is a difficult question: to what extent did *The Waste Land*, an international sensation, shape the rest of Eliot's life and work? The poem is *not* a conversionary work, unlike *Ash Wednesday* (1930). It is a text of personal breakdown and poetic crisis, covertly taking Walt Whitman's "When Lilacs Last in the Dooryard Bloom'd" as its paradigm. Time very likely will demonstrate that Eliot's deepest poetic affinities were with Whitman and Tennyson, and not with Baudelaire and Dante.

Doubtless more definitive biographies of T.S. Eliot will be written: thousands of his letters are sequestered, and his widow, Valerie Eliot, is the keeper of the Flame. Incomplete information will some day be filled out. Our views of his life will alter. The earlier poetry, one can prophesy, will retain its pungency. Acrid and eloquent, it created the style of its Age.

ELLYN SANNA

Biography of T.S. Eliot

An Extraordinary Bank Clerk

From all outward appearances, T.S. Eliot seemed a quiet, straight-forward bank clerk. But like Kafka, Melville, and countless other writers, Eliot lived a distinctly separate literary life—a life of the mind. While quietly working as an unremarkable clerk, he produced some of the century's greatest poetry.

T.S. Eliot worked for the prestigious Lloyd's of London Bank, where he excelled as a clerk while maintaining the personal distance necessary to create his verse. His office was in the cellars, beneath London's pavement, and the only noise that disturbed his thoughts was the constant tapping of pedestrians' feet on the green glass cubes of the walk just above his head. Hidden away in quiet dusty rooms, Eliot prepared wills and tidied up estates with careful efficiency. These endless, precise tasks left his imagination free to wander down more creative paths, and acted as a strategy of sorts, allowing the poet an insider's view of typical American daily labor. Clerking afforded him the opportunity to work amongst "the termites."

Eliot's wife, Vivienne, urged her husband to find a more literary job, something that would make him more visible as a poet. "What's the use of being famous after you're dead?" she asked him. But Eliot refused. He was comfortable at the bank; his salary there increased steadily, providing him with a secure income; and he did not want to compromise his writing by having to depend on it for income. His bank job left him free to write only what he wanted, with all the creative liberation he desired.

Eliot's aim was to compose an extended collection of poems that would denounce modern civilization and capture the disillusionment of his postwar generation. From the quiet distance of his bank clerk veil, he wrote about society with scornful power. Modern poetry had struck its note. *The Waste Land*, published in 1922, transformed Eliot into a successful poet. The American first edition promptly sold out and had to be reissued almost immediately. The book won the prestigious Dial Award; eventually, it would make T.S. Eliot's name well known to millions of people.

But Eliot the man wasn't ready to make a break from his everyday life. He continued to work at Lloyd's, where his employers were pleased, if mystified, by his literary success. One of the bank's officers declared:

> You know, I myself am really very glad indeed to hear [that Eliot is a good poet]. Many of my colleagues wouldn't agree at all. They think a Banker has no business whatever to be a poet.... But I believe that anything a man does, whatever his *hobby* may be, it's all the better if he is really keen on it and does it well.... In fact, if he goes on as he has been doing, I don't see why—in time, of course, in time—he mightn't even become a Branch Manager.

Of course, poetry was far more than a mere hobby for Eliot, and his aspirations ran further than Lloyd's of London. Banking might have been his day job, but poetry was his life.

Eliot was indeed attached to his carefully constructed personae, which had more attractions than the steady income. His family, who all had busy successful careers of their own, approved of his job, and Eliot, who had always been considered taciturn, hated to alienate himself from them any more than he already had. Eventually, masquerading between tormented poet and bourgeoisie banker began to take its toll. Eliot wanted to reveal his true self to those closest to him. Exposing the genuine T.S. Eliot—even to himself—was a long journey.

THE SAFETY OF HOME

From the beginning, Thomas Stearns Eliot was different from the rest of his family, if only because he was so much younger. He was born on

September 26, 1888, in St. Louis, Missouri, the seventh child of a New England schoolteacher and a St. Louis merchant, both of whom were middle-aged by the time their last child was born. The Eliots were one of St. Louis's most respected families; they were part of the elite group that gave the city a unique cultural tone, descended from a long line of ministers and merchants. John Quincy Adams was a distant relation.

Although Eliot was the youngest of a large family and in temperament more sensitive than his siblings, his position in the family was an important one. He was never regarded as an afterthought. Instead, his family, particularly his mother, taught him that he was exceptional. Since his brothers and sisters were all quite a bit older, Eliot spent much of his time alone, reading. Yet Eliot, reticent by nature, preferred this solitary pursuit to socializing; even at a young age, his introversion created distance between himself and others.

His mother, Charlotte Champe Eliot, was one of his only companions. She spoke to her youngest son as an equal, a habit that must have taught Eliot self-respect from an early age. Charlotte had strong morals and high ideals; she taught her children to work hard every day to become better people, "to make the best of every faculty and control every evil."

But Charlotte was also protective of Eliot and kept him from participating in football and other sports. He had been born with a double hernia, and she feared if he exerted himself, the hernia would rupture. She accompanied him on every outing to make sure he did not become too cold or wet, too hot or tired. Eliot apparently did not resent his mother, and as an adult, he expressed to her his "infinite love." Her hovering presence, however, separated him from other children his own age, and her influence on his attitude toward women and life was at times overwhelming.

Charlotte's control over her son may have been influenced by her own thwarted ambitions. She recognized in Eliot some of her own dreams and talents. She had longed to be a poet, but she had been held back by the traditions of the day that insisted a woman could not pursue higher education. In Eliot, Charlotte saw a chance to vicariously achieve her abandoned ambition.

Although she could not devote her life to intellectual pursuits, Charlotte did continue to write poetry, and her work undoubtedly influenced her son. Her works deal with the role of the seer or prophet, the thinker whose private vision benefits the rest of society. Although her words were often trite, her son would later express many of her themes and images with greater lucidity and vividness. The questions Eliot would ask in his own poetry were not new to him as an adult, for his mother had taught them to him from childhood: How does a person face annihilation? Is life worth living when we know we must die? Is this life all that we are offered?

Charlotte was both deeply intellectual and intensely spiritual, traits she passed to her youngest son. In her room she hung religious paintings to remind her that the spiritual world's power is greater than that of the temporal world around us. Withheld by her role as wife and mother from a life more focused on spiritual and intellectual concerns, she expressed her deepest interests not only through motherhood but by participating in local social reforms; she fought for better conditions for women prisoners and a better justice system for juveniles.

Eliot's father probably had less influence over his son. Henry Ware Eliot Sr. was a refined man who loved music and art. His own father had hoped Henry would follow in the family tradition and become a clergyman, but Henry had rebelled. He said of his father's efforts to influence the shape of his life, "Too much pudding choked the dog," and Henry instead became successful as a manufacturer of bricks. Despite his choice of profession, Henry remained a deeply moral man, with a puritanical outlook on sexuality. During Eliot's childhood, his father was often preoccupied with business and responsibility, but Henry also had streaks of whimsy—he liked to draw faces on his children's boiled eggs—as well as idiosyncrasy—he had an odd habit of smelling his food before he ate it. He spoke of his youngest son as a modest and affectionate boy, but not a promising one, since his school grades were mediocre; as a youngster, his father's assessment of him left Eliot with a "mournful" feeling.

Because of industries like Henry Ware Eliot's, at the turn of the century the city of St. Louis was not a particularly beautiful place: its sewers were inadequate for the factories' waste products, and the air was filled with sulfur fumes. The stench of pollution did not stick in Eliot's mind, though, when he looked back at his childhood. Instead, later in life he said, "I am very well satisfied with having been born in St. Louis." Instead of industrial scenes, Eliot remembered the ever-present Mississippi River always in the background of his life as a child. "I feel that there is something in having passed one's childhood beside the big river," he wrote in 1930, "which is incommunicable to those who have not."

Eliot also recalled from his childhood his Irish nurse, Annie Dunne, who often went to pray in a small Catholic church. When Eliot was six years old, Annie discussed with him the existence of God. She not only stimulated his early religious thinking, giving him a glimpse of liturgical Christianity so different from Eliot's own Unitarian background, but she also made him feel secure; he would later confess that he was "greatly attached" to her.

The Eliot family did not spend all their time in St. Louis; they vacationed on Cape Ann in northern Massachusetts, and when Eliot was eight, his father built the family a large house beside the ocean, near Gloucester. From the house's windows, Eliot could look out at the fishing fleet's white sails in the harbor. From Gloucester's fishermen, Eliot learned a respect for heroism and self-reliance. The fisherman's perilous existence spoke to his imagination and influenced the metaphors he used later in life when he wrote *The Waste Land* and *Four Quartets*.

Eliot himself became a competent sailor, and despite fog and rough waves, some of his happiest hours growing up were spent off the New England coast. He explored the Cape Ann beaches, finding bits and pieces of ocean treasures—a starfish, a whale bone, a broken oar, a horseshoe crab, images he later included in "Dry Salvages," one of the poems that makes up *Four Quartets*. When he was 10, he found a sea anemone in a tidal pool, an experience that impressed him deeply. The still pool filled with light became a recurring image for the tantalizing memory of something wonderful.

Eliot attended Miss Locke's Primary School in St. Louis, and then went on to enter Smith Academy. His first poems and prose pieces appeared in the *Smith Academy Record* in 1915, the year of his graduation. He spent the last year of his high school education at Milton Academy, a private prep school in Massachusetts.

When Eliot was 16, his mother published a biography of her father-in-law, William Greenleaf Eliot. She dedicated it to her children with the inscription "Lest They Forget." Eliot's grandfather had been a prominent Unitarian minister who had dedicated his life to improving the world; during the 1849 cholera epidemic in St. Louis, William

Greenleaf Eliot visited the sick and dying for weeks on end, sleeping so little that his right hand became permanently paralyzed as a result of his exhaustion. Although this patriarch died before his youngest grandson's birth, his virtues continued to be held up as a model to the younger generation. Eliot later recalled of his grandfather: "I was brought up to be very much aware of him. The standard of conduct was that which my grandfather had set: our moral judgments, our decisions between duty and self-indulgence, were taken as if, like Moses, he had brought down the tables of the Law, and deviation from which would be sinful...." William Greenleaf Eliot was not an easy model for Eliot to follow.

Charlotte admired her father-in-law, and she particularly emphasized two of his "laws" to her children: self-denial and public service. As an adult, Eliot acknowledged that this early emphasis on self-denial left him unable to enjoy even harmless pleasures without a sense of guilt. For instance, his mother taught him that eating candy was self-indulgent and the practice of self-denial was crucial to overall physical health. Not until his 60s, when he was forced to give up smoking for health reasons, could he bring himself to eat candy, and then only as a substitute for smoking. But his grandfather's other precept—public service—acted a bit differently on Eliot. It gave him a strong sense of mission.

Eliot was to express this sense of mission differently than the rest of his family. The members of his family were busy with actively bettering the world through professions like teaching, doctoring, and preaching. Eliot was not well suited to these active careers. Instead, he longed to express in a different way his mission to change the world for the better.

In his poem "Animula," Eliot describes a young person who experiences a tug-of-war between dreams and the call to take action in the busy world. As a young adult, Eliot felt this same conflict. On the one hand, he wanted to be a poet—but on the other, he hated to ignore his upbringing, which pressured him to do something concrete for society. As he grew up, he worried about what his family would think of his career. "No man wholly escapes from the kind," he wrote, "or wholly surpasses the degree, of culture which he acquired from his early environment."

By the time Eliot left home to attend Harvard, he had been deeply saturated in the religious values of his family. The religion passed along by his grandfather, however, had more to do with morals than any deep awareness of spiritual things, and this sort of religion failed to stimulate Eliot's imagination. Although his mother may have possessed a private spirituality, Eliot later recalled that his parents did not talk of good and evil but of what was "done" and "not done."

His family belonged to the Unitarian church, a form of religion that was confident of humanity's nobility. The Unitarians rejected the Puritans' wrathful God who would punish sinful humans. Instead, Unitarians stressed the power of human beings to bring about good for themselves. They were called Unitarians because they did not believe in the doctrine of the Trinity, and they had little faith in the concept of Christ as God in a human body. Human beings did not need to rely for their redemption on Christ, the Unitarians asserted; instead, their church optimistically claimed that human progress would continue eternally.

Eliot ultimately rejected the religion in which he was raised. His fervent nature found no nourishment in Unitarianism and he began to search for an older, stricter discipline, unsoftened by nineteenth-century liberalism. By the time he left for Harvard in 1906, he had become completely indifferent to the church.

THE HARVARD YEARS

Harvard's Boston had little to feed Eliot's hungry imagination. The city's early Puritan core had been displaced by enormous businesses and industries. The social class that grew out of this commercial wealth was proud and preoccupied with its own affairs; its members spent their time observing each other and gossiping. Later, Eliot would write of his time in Boston: "We looked through each other like microscopes.... Unitarianism kept us all shallow. We knew nothing—no! but really nothing! of the world.... God knows that we knew our want of knowledge! the self-knowledge became introspection—nervous self-consciousness...."

Disillusioned with his own social class, Eliot turned instead to Boston's slums. Growing up in St. Louis, he had never been exposed to that city's poor areas, but now he deliberately sought out Boston's uglier streets. There he found broken glass and dirty windows, trampled mud and debris-filled vacant lots. As an adult, he said that "the contemplation of the horrid or sordid or disgusting by an artist, is the necessary and negative aspect of the impulse toward the pursuit of beauty." He was depressed and repelled by the ugliness, but he was also moved and attracted. From these scenes he began to build the image of the wasteland that would later be so important to his poetry, evident in such early poems as "The Preludes."

His studies at Harvard did not fascinate him nearly as much as he had expected, nor did the campus social life. Eliot roomed with a plump friend, Howard Morris, who loved eating and drinking far better than reading. Eliot had little in common with his roommate, but free from the confines of home, he forced himself to participate in some of the students' social activities. Most people, however, perceived him to be a shy and studious recluse.

The intellectual scene at Harvard was little better than the social one. Charles W. Eliot, a relative, was the president of Harvard during his years there, but this distant kinsman encouraged an atmosphere of coolness and distance at the university. There was little exchange of ideas, and the professors tended to be snobbish and stand-offish, while the students lived in separate dwellings and socialized only at clubs. President Eliot focused the university's attention on science, while he considered the humanities to be a subject good only for women to study. "Art is left to languish and die," wrote Eliot's brother Henry, and his cousin Fred Eliot added, "The study of classics is practically dead at Harvard." Literature did not make people rich; it did not build anything; and it did not win wars. In President Eliot's eyes, it was simply not man's work.

But two of T.S. Eliot's professors looked at things differently; Irving Babbitt and George Santayana had enormous influence on Eliot's development. Both men impressed on Eliot their criticism of America's political scene. Santayana had rejected Catholicism, but he told his students that the Catholic Church was the only remaining keeper of the treasures of the past. This line of thinking appealed to Eliot, as did Babbitt's emphasis on the dangers of the modern secular world. Babbitt was also interested in Eastern philosophy; this and other aspects of Babbitt's teaching spoke to Eliot's imagination. The themes of eastern philosophy was to appear in several of his poems, including the opening to the third section of "The Dry Salvages":

I sometimes wonder if that is what Krishna meant—
Among other things—or one way of putting the same thing:
That the future is a faded song, a Royal Rose or a lavender
   spray
Of wistful regret for those who are not yet here to regret,
Pressed between yellow leaves of a book that has never been
   opened.

Ultimately, Eliot rejected Babbitt's humanism and lack of faith, but he still acknowledged the imprint his old professor left on his thinking. In 1941, Eliot wrote of Babbitt, "Even in the convictions one may feel, the views one may hold, that seem to contradict most important convictions of Babbitt's own, one is aware that he himself was very largely the cause of them. The magnitude of the debt that some of us owe to him should be more obvious to posterity than to our contemporaries."

Eliot did make one close friend during his Harvard years—the author Conrad Aiken, who was also a student. The two young men were both editors of the *Harvard Advocate*, and they shared many interests. They were very different from each other, however, when it came to women: Conrad Aiken was obsessed with them, while Eliot had problems relating to the opposite sex. Despite their differences, Aiken's friendship was good for Eliot. Aiken, who called Eliot by the nickname "Tsetse," kept Eliot from becoming too withdrawn, and he encouraged Eliot's literary talents.

During his Harvard years, Eliot had already begun writing poetry. He did not try to publish these verses until years later, but instead he collected them in a notebook which he titled *Inventions of the March Hare*. The title tells something about how Eliot perceived his thinking; although he took his internal life very seriously, he knew it was at odds with the rest of the world.

In an environment where most people were busy with practical affairs, Eliot was instead deeply immersed in a spiritual quest—his religious thinking was slowly taking shape throughout his university years. He later wrote, "Towards any profound conviction one is borne gradually, perhaps insensibly over a long period of time." He became fascinated with the concepts of the "Absolute" and the "Soul," and he believed that women, time, and society were the enemies of this

Absolute. Eliot called on the Absolute to rescue the soul from the "mud of physical sense." However, it is important to note that Eliot scrupulously acknowledged the pomposity of this ideal and always guarded it with a mocking humor.

Eliot's difficulties with women emerged during his college years. The women he had known growing up—his mother, his older sister Ada, and his Boston cousins Martha and Abigail—were all strong, intelligent, active women; and yet for some reason Eliot developed a quite different image of females as a whole. Perhaps the strength and protectiveness of the real-life women in his family had threatened his sense of his own identity. At any rate, his poetry described women as pale, fragile, and shallow; his fictional women devoured energy, sapped strength, and emasculated men.

Eliot may also have been uncomfortable with women because he was uneasy with his own sexuality. In his mind, the material world, the world we perceive with our senses, was a threat to the ideal world of the Absolute. He felt that his own physical life was an embarrassing distraction from his spiritual identity, and during these years he saw his body as the enemy of his soul.

Eliot came by these feelings honestly. His mother had written poetry that called for the reader to "loose the spirit from its mesh, / From the poor vesture of the flesh," and his father was quite frank about his belief that sex was simply "nastiness." Henry Ware Sr. considered sex education for children to be a "letter of introduction to the Devil." He viewed syphilis as God's punishment for sexual promiscuity, and he devoutly hoped that a cure for the disease would never be found. If it were, he said, it might be necessary to "emasculate our children to keep them clean."

Attitudes like these shaped Eliot's thinking. The poems he wrote during these years connect sexual love with violence, sin, and death. Throughout his life, the women he described in his writing were flat, two-dimensional shapes, stereotypical saints or sinners whose only threat to the masculine world was the allure of their bodies.

Feelings like these made the young student feel out of place in the world around him, but his confusion was soon to be shaped by another influence. In December 1908, Eliot picked up a book from the Harvard library that showed him a new way of looking at his own intrinsic life. The book was Arthur Symons's *The Symbolist Movement in Literature*, and it called for artists to take up a spiritual vision. According to Symons, the poet's sacred task was to free himself of the "old bondage of exteriority" and become a prophet of the unknown—even if this freedom came close to madness. The artist, said Symons, is a seer, a prophet, someone with a childlike vision who stands apart from the adult world of material concerns. Art, which becomes religion, wrote Symons, may be an escape from time and mortality.

Eliot seized on this philosophy with joy and relief. It echoed ideas he had learned from his mother, and it made sense out of his own longings. Symons's book introduced Eliot to an intellectual world where he was no longer alone, for it was inhabited by others like himself, including the French poets Laforgue and Baudelaire.

Eliot eagerly began reading Laforgue's poetry. From the French writer he learned the technique of using a central persona in his own poems, a clown or marionette who is trapped in a silly role, an outcast who is unable to take command of his real self. But while the French poets shared Eliot's sense of looking at both the self and society from a disillusioned distance, Laforgue and Baudelaire's attitudes were far more tolerant than Eliot's.

Eliot's loathing for both himself and the world around him continued to grow. He wrote of himself:

> How unpleasant to meet Mr. Eliot!
> With his features of so clerical cut,
> And his brow so grim
> And his mouth so prim
> And his conversation, so nicely
> Restricted to What Precisely
> And If and Perhaps and But.

Despite Eliot's awareness of his own prim and sometimes unappealing image, he continued to cultivate a precise, exterior style, a way of maintaining distance from others. He thought of Laforgue as his older brother, he commented later, and he admired Laforgue's public image—a dandy with perfect dress and manners. Eliot went so far as to intentionally make Laforgue's persona his own. Aikens wrote of his friend, "Manners is an obsolete word nowadays, but he had them."

In his poetry, Eliot described himself as the "first born child of the Absolute, / turned out neatly in a flannel suit." He used a similar image in an early poem called "Spleen," where he describes himself as

... Languid, fastidious, and bland,
Waits, hat and gloves in hand,
Punctilious of tie and suit
(Somewhat impatient of delay)
On the doorstep of the Absolute.

At last, in the summer of 1911, Eliot perfected this prim and fastidious poetic version of himself when he created Prufrock, the central character in "The Love Song of J. Alfred Prufrock."

Eliot was in the process of defining his own character—but the identity he was formulating was still not comfortable in the world where he lived. He was tired of Harvard's emptiness: the endless and pointless debates, the flirtations, the academic boredom. Most of all, he was tired of his own family's expectations.

As Eliot neared the end of his college years, his parents were eager to know what career he would choose. They expected him to carry on the Eliot legacy by taking up some profession that would improve human society in a concrete and practical way. His older siblings and cousins were all settling nicely into their public-spirited careers: his sisters Ada and Marian were social workers; his cousin Martha was studying to be a doctor; her sister Abigail was going into education (the school she eventually founded would be a precursor of the "Head Start" program for underprivileged children); and Eliot had two other cousins who were studying to be clergymen. But Eliot had no interest in pursuing any of these noble professions. Instead, he wanted to go to Paris.

His parents could not understand why he would want to go to such a faraway and corrupt city. His mother wrote to him in April 1910:

I suppose you will know better in June what you want to do next year.... I cannot bear to think of your being alone in Paris, the very words give me a chill. English-speaking countries seem so different from foreign. I do not admire the French nation, and have less confidence in individuals of that race than in English.

Eliot insisted, however, that he did indeed want to go to France; he felt certain that in Paris he would find a place where he would fit in better, a place where he would find the intellectual and artistic stimulation he craved. In May, however, Eliot fell ill with what may have been scarlet fever. He was hospitalized, and his mother rushed from St. Louis to nurse him back to health. Although he soon recovered, his plans for going abroad were temporarily dismissed.

About the time of his graduation from Harvard in June 1910, Eliot had a metaphysical experience, a pivotal moment in his life. As he was walking through Boston one day, the busy streets suddenly seemed to shrink away, leaving him wrapped in a great silence that was both comforting and terrifying. "You may call it communion with the Divine," he wrote later, "or you may call it temporary crystallization of the mind." The experience inspired him to write a poem titled "Silence," and he spent much of his life trying to recall the moment when everything else in life had dropped away, leaving him at peace.

Eliot was still seeking a religious identity, but this experience helped him to be certain of at least one thing: he did not belong in Boston. To Eliot, Paris meant a place where, as a poet, he might feel less at odds with society, and he probably dreamed, like any provincial, of belonging in a great center of artistic and intellectual innovation. To the average American, however, Paris was for tourists and expatriated bohemians. American men simply did not go there seriously to live. Despite his family's objections, Eliot would go to Paris.

A LONELY MAN

In 1910, Eliot crossed the Atlantic to what he hoped would be a Paris filled with the spiritual malaise and morbidity of the poets he admired. He had planned to immerse himself in the city, and even thought he would gradually give up English and write in French instead.

But Eliot did not find the intellectual and artistic refuge he had hoped for. The poetry he wrote during his year in Paris suggests that he felt more isolated and hopeless than ever. After a few months, he was as disillusioned with the French city as he had been with Boston. He felt weighted down by French society's indulgent sophistication and decadence of the infamous Montparnasse Quarter. The women, the food, the smoke of cigars left him feeling empty and bored.

But in Paris he again experienced "a ring of silence" that closed around him like a chrysalis. He sensed that his soul both longed for and feared the winged freedom that waited for it. Later, he would give these feelings a religious interpretation, but at this point of his life he resisted any implication that God was involved in the experience. He connected God with his family's cheery moral religion—and the duty that held no appeal for him.

Just as he had in Boston, he began to hunt out the darker, seamier neighborhoods in Paris. He explored the streets at night, when the prostitutes and drunks walked the alleys, and he took a perverse pleasure in contemplating human beings who lived without morals or dignity.

Eliot wrote poems about these experiences, while he also continued to write about his own interior world. His writing seemed to him to be mere fragments, however, and he longed to fit his poems into an overarching framework, a unified way of looking at life. By the summer of 1911, he had decided to return to Harvard to study philosophy. Through critical examination of fundamental beliefs, he hoped philosophy would afford him the opportunity for extended self reflection and give him the answers he was seeking.

Still feeling desperately alone, he returned to Harvard that fall. His poetry expressed his longing for just one person to understand his feelings, even if it were a stranger he met on the stairs or passed on the street. His friend Conrad Aiken described the way he once more tried to fit into Harvard's social scene: "He was early explicit, too, about the necessity, if one was shy, of disciplining oneself, lest one miss certain varieties of experience which one did not naturally 'take' to. The dances, and the parties, were a part of this discipline, as ... was his taking boxing lessons." Despite his efforts, though, Eliot's time back in Harvard was filled with distress. Night after night, he lay awake, plagued with panic attacks and a despair that was nearly suicidal.

He was not finding the answers he had hoped to encounter in the study of philosophy. Unfortunately, he had returned to Harvard just as the university's best philosophy professors—Santayana and Henry James—left the department. Instead, Eliot studied under Bertrand Russell, but he could not accept that Russell's philosophy had "anything to do with reality." Eliot did, however, discover the writings of one philosopher with whom he could identify: F.H. Bradley.

In Bradley, Eliot found someone who was asking the same questions about life as he was: Is the universe concealed behind appearances? Is ultimate reality and the physical world linked together in any way? What is the connection between individual experience and the Absolute? As he studied Bradley's metaphysical work, Eliot felt less estranged from the rest of the world.

Bradley, however, was more hopeful than Eliot. The older thinker was convinced that the concrete world and the Absolute were somehow joined; ultimate reality was the "underlying harmony" that gave the physical world meaning. Eliot longed for this same understanding, but in the end, he rejected Bradley's views. For Eliot, his own consciousness—even his dreams and hallucinations—were more important than the concrete world around him. With a deep despair, his poetry acknowledged that he was edging dangerously close to madness.

He turned to Eastern philosophy, relieved to encounter religious beliefs that were refreshingly different from his family's. He also memorized long passages of Dante's *Divine Comedy*, finding comfort in Dante's view of hell and redemption. And he studied the lives of the saints and mystics, trying to understand the meaning of their visions. He wrote a series of poems that focused on religious experiences.

While Eliot's interior life was still consumed by uncertainty and fear, on the outside he became a bit less isolated. He had returned from Paris with a polished, European air that helped give him confidence in social settings. Struggling to fit in, he even enrolled in dancing and skating lessons, and he wrote crude verses for the entertainment of his friends. He attended recitals and operas, and was elected president of Harvard's Philosophical Society.

In the winter of 1913, Eliot acted in a variety show in the house of his aunt. Another actor in the show, Emily Hale, was a friend of his cousin, and Eliot and Emily became close friends. Many surmise that they may have fallen in love at that time, but this was never confirmed; the details of their relationship remain a mystery. He and Hale started a correspondence that lasted over the course of their lives, but their friendship wasn't to be revived for several years.

While Eliot was finding ways to fit in externally, he continued to be uncomfortable with his intellectual life. He was no longer satisfied with his poetry; "I know the kind of verse I want," he wrote to Aiken, "and I know this isn't it.... I shan't do anything that will satisfy me (as my old stuff *does* satisfy me) for years."

Frustrated, Eliot gave up on Harvard and went back to Europe. He had intended to study in Germany, but on August 14, right after his arrival, war broke out. Eliot had arrived there just in time for the beginning of what was then known at the Great War, what we today call World War I. To escape the conflict, Eliot retreated to England and entered Oxford Univsersity.

At Oxford, Eliot continued to study philosophy and worked on his doctoral dissertation on Bradley. Meanwhile, his parents were pressuring him to come home; they wanted him to abandon his intellectual and spiritual pursuits and take up a practical career. At his parents' urging, he finished his doctoral dissertation and submitted it to Harvard, but he never completed his degree. He had no interest in becoming a professor, but he did not know how to withstand his parents' pressure to make him conform to their image. Eliot needed an excuse for staying in England, away from his family's shadow.

He wrote little poetry during these years, and he continued to struggle with his sense of alienation from the rest of the world. Despite his isolation, he felt a sudden impulse "to be a moment merry," he wrote to Aiken in 1914. He was ready to have women fall in love with him, he told his friend. At last, he could no longer bear his ongoing retreat from the world, and he took a desperate leap toward involvement with other human beings. The following spring, he met Vivienne Haigh-Wood and two months later, in June 1915, they were married. Now Eliot had an excuse for not going home to the United States and his family.

Vivienne was a governess with a Cambridge family, but she was interested in the arts. Her father was a painter, and she herself painted, wrote poetry and prose, and studied ballet. She liked to wear bright colors and dramatic clothes; Eliot admired her honesty and daring. Vivienne was wild and mercurial, a world apart from Eliot's serious mother. As an Englishwoman, she was a mystery to Eliot, who may not have known what to make of her staring eyes and open mouth. Her impulsiveness, her smoking and dancing, and her eloquent intelligence teased his cautious nature. Not least of Vivienne's attractions was her faith in Eliot as an upcoming poet. She was not the sort of woman of whom his mother would have approved, but that may have been part of her attraction for Eliot. Perhaps he married her so quickly and without the knowledge of either set of parents because he was afraid if he hesitated he would never dare to act at all. Later he wrote that it was better to do wrong than to do nothing at all: "at least we exist." He wanted to escape from his endless doubts and fears, and plunge into the "real" world. Unfortunately, Eliot was not prepared for such a plunge.

In London, Eliot had struck up a friendship with his former professor Bertrand Russell, and Russell became a confidant for the young couple. Eliot's mother wrote to Russell, urging him to encourage her son to choose "Philosophy as a life work.... I had hoped he would seek a University appointment next year." Charlotte could accept her son being a philosophy professor, but she was not comfortable with him being a poet. Besides, she wanted him to come home.

But marriage meant that Eliot had to support a wife, and he settled for teaching at Highgate Junior School, where he taught French, Latin, lower mathematics, drawing, swimming, geography, history, and baseball. Eliot did not enjoy the work, and it has been speculated the couple may not have had enough money to move back to America. Bertrand Russell, however, suspected that Vivienne was afraid to meet Eliot's family, and Eliot was still not eager to go home where he would be expected to abide by the conventions of his family's world.

His reluctance to face his family, however, was not a good foundation on which to build a marriage. On a Friday evening, only a month after their wedding, while the young couple entertained Russell over dinner, Vivienne confided that she had married her husband to stimulate him, but she had found she was unable to do so. Eliot said nothing.

A year or so after their wedding, Eliot wrote that he had been through the "most awful nightmare of anxiety that the mind of man could conceive." The very things that had first attracted him to Vivienne—her brash honesty and loud, uninhibited voice—now repelled him. His friends could see that he was ashamed of his new wife. He did not know how to handle her wild emotions, and she did not understand his inhibitions and shyness.

Russell continued to take the young couple under his wing. He even invited them to live in his London apartment, and since they were desperately poor, they accepted his invitation. He was fond of them both and wrote of Eliot,

It is quite funny how I have come to love him, as if he were my son. He is becoming much more of a man. He has a profound and quite unselfish devotion to his wife, and she is really quite fond of him, but has impulses of cruelty to him from time to time.... She is a person who lives on a knife-edge, and will end as a criminal or a saint—I don't know which yet. She has a perfect capacity for both.

Perhaps in some ways, Eliot and his new wife were too much alike. They were both plagued with neuroses, prone to panic attacks and fits of depression. But while Eliot carefully contained his emotions within the distant persona he had created, Vivienne vented every feeling that passed through her. She screamed and sobbed and raged. Living with her must have been exhausting for Eliot.

He soon found that his new wife was also a sickly woman who spent her life in a constant cycle of health crises and convalescence. Her frequent "nervous collapses" were brought on by severe headaches, and her family did little to help her. The task of doctoring her fell on Eliot.

Both Eliot and his wife wrote of their marriage as a cage, a trap they could not escape. For Vivienne, the cage represented her loneliness, but for Eliot it was the opposite—the constant lack of privacy, the way an animal in the zoo has nowhere to go to escape the eyes of its observers. "It is terrible," he wrote, "to be alone with another person."

From 1917 to 1919, Eliot served as assistant editor of the *Egoist*, where he published some of his criticism. Two important factors in Eliot's development as a poet were his introduction to French symbolist poetry and his friendship with fellow expatriate American Ezra Pound. It was in Pound that Eliot found a devoted mentor and a sensitive critic of the early drafts of his poems. Pound set himself to grooming the younger poet, and he also concerned himself with the practical details of Eliot's life. Without Eliot's knowledge, Pound even personally borrowed money to pay for the printing of Eliot's first book, *The Love Song of J. Alfred Prufrock and Other Observations*. "Prufrock" is a long dramatic monologue about a fastidious middle-aged man who is unable to overcome his emotional timidity to find love and meaning in life; his frustrations reflect the dilemmas of modern society, especially middle-class culture.

Pound encouraged Eliot's rejection of America. Their home country, Pound wrote, was infected with "blood poison," and Eliot had the disease "worse than I have—poor devil." Encouraged by his new sponsor, Eliot settled himself in England. After all, he had never really belonged in his own country.

Eliot had been writing religious poetry again when he first met Pound, but the older poet had no time for Christianity. Pound persuaded Eliot to turn back to social commentary. The poems Eliot wrote during this time were bitter and sarcastic. He kept his thoughts hidden from Pound, but Eliot continued to brood about Christianity. As always, he was full of doubts, but, he later said, a "doubter is a man who takes the problem of his faith seriously." By July 1917, he was forced to acknowledge that without faith he felt his life was poor and barren—and yet he was still not convinced that religion was worth all the effort it demanded.

But Eliot's life continued to be filled with difficulty and trauma. In order to survive emotionally, he desperately needed a way to make sense out of all his doubts and depression. The Eliots' marriage had continued to deteriorate. When Eliot discovered that Vivienne had had a brief affair with Bertrand Russell, he was disillusioned with both his wife and his friend. His poetry reflected his bitterness:

> I have lost my passion: why should I need to keep it
> When what is kept must be adulterated?

The women he portrayed in his poems were increasingly predatory— barren, sickly parasites who offered men nothing but trials.

The couple also had financial worries. Eliot gave up teaching and instead worked as a bank clerk, a job to which he was better suited temperamentally. Still, he was often so short of money that he was forced to ask his parents for help. He did not turn to his in-laws, however; the Haigh-Woods had made clear that they could do nothing for the young couple.

The Eliots were still trying to persuade their son to come home to Boston, but he continued to find reasons for staying in England. The war was the best reason, of course, since travel was unsafe if not impossible. He also used Vivienne's poor health as an excuse. As a result, his parents were not inclined to approve of his new wife. They suspected that she was extravagant, since Eliot asked for increasingly large sums to help him deal with his wife's frequent illnesses.

Vivienne's letters to her in-laws tried to reassure their suspicions; she insisted that the doctor had told her that her migraines were caused by starvation, and that he had ordered her to refrain from economizing. Vivienne also told Eliot's mother that she was exhausted from darning her husband's worn-out underwear—and then Vivienne tried to explain why she needed new clothes for a visit to wealthy friends.

The Eliots were not impressed with the image they shaped of their daughter-in-law. Henry Ware Eliot Sr. was convinced that his son had wrecked his life. Before his death in January 1919, Eliot's father made legal arrangements that would ensure Vivienne would receive nothing from an Eliot inheritance. Eliot's mother had a softer approach, but she too disapproved of her son's marriage and lifestyle. She was sorry that he needed to work so hard at a job he didn't like—"it is like putting Pegasus into a harness," she wrote—but she decided that his inability to take on a "real" profession stemmed from the fact that she had overprotected him in the past. Now, she told him, he would have to make his own way.

To please his mother, Eliot tried to enlist in the U.S. navy. Charlotte was a vehement supporter of the war; she had been writing newspaper letters for years, urging Americans to get involved in the war, and she had also written a war song for the Boston *Herald*. Eliot too felt a sense of duty toward the armed services and he hoped that the navy might give him a sense of belonging and more freedom to write. However, he was disqualified from active service because of a rapid heartbeat and his old hernia. He tried to join the U.S. Intelligence, but again he was rejected.

These rejections only hardened his feelings of resentment toward his home country. Americans were immature, he concluded, and he began to shift his allegiance to England. "The *intelligent* Englishman is more aware of loneliness," he wrote, "has more reserves, than the man of intelligence of any other nation." England, he decided, would be his new homeland.

This new allegiance was strengthened when he became acquainted with a group of English writers, the Bloomsbury Group. The author Virginia Woolf was an important part of this literary circle. She and the other authors were a liberal, relaxed, bohemian group, and they often made fun of Eliot's stern and proper air, but gradually they came to accept and respect him. Their friendship helped shape his career as a poet.

In May 1919, Leonard and Virginia Woolf produced a collection of Eliot's poems, *Poems 1919*, at their small publishing house, Hogarth Press. A year later Alfred Knopf, an American publisher, published *Poems by T. S. Eliot* in the United States, while the same collection came out in London under the title *Ara Vos Prec*. Soon after, a collection of Eliot's essays, *The Sacred Wood*, was also published.

As a poet, Eliot was becoming famous—but his private life was still miserable. Still, he reasoned, he would use the pain of his personal life as fuel for his poetry. He told his friend Aiken that he had "*lived* through material for a score of long poems in the last six months." He resolved to write a long poem—*The Waste Land*, the work that would ultimately become his most famous.

A TROUBLED LIFE

Although Eliot decided to write *The Waste Land* at the end of 1919, throughout the following year he did nothing to follow through with his plan. He was too busy with his personal affairs.

In the fall of 1920, his father-in-law became critically ill, and Vivienne and Eliot sat up together, night after night, nursing him. Vivienne broke down under the strain, and throughout the spring of 1921 she suffered pain so intense that she screamed endlessly for days at a time. Eliot realized that his home would never be magically transformed into a peaceful place where he would have quiet and leisure to compose poetry. Instead, if he were to survive emotionally and spiritually, he would need to create a mental sanctuary for himself. He turned once more to his writing. During this period he wrote the first drafts of parts one and two of *The Waste Land*.

His creative work was interrupted, however, by a visit from his mother, sister, and brother. He had not seen his mother in six years, and he feared he would find her old and weak, since she was now 77. Instead, he was overwhelmed by her energy. Just as she had when he was a child, Charlotte longed to protect him and set his world right. Trying to keep his marital problems under wraps from his mother's sharp intuition, Eliot grew more and more tense.

Vivienne tried hard to cooperate with her husband's efforts to put on a good front for his family. She stayed in the country for much of the Eliots' visit, and she worked hard to maintain a cool, composed manner whenever she was in their presence. At the end of their visit, however, her composure slipped so far that she threw a hysterical fit. Later, in a letter to her brother-in-law, she apologized for the fact "that I behaved like 'no lady,' and just like a wild animal."

Her in-laws were horrified by Vivienne's behavior. Eliot's brother Henry wrote to his mother later,

> I have a feeling that subconsciously (or unconsciously) she likes the role of invalid, and that, liking it as she does to be petted, "made a fuss over," condoled and consoled, she ... encourages her breakdowns, instead of throwing them off by a sort of nervous resistance. It is hard to tell how much is physical; but I think that if she had more of "the Will to Be Well" she would have less suffering.... She needs something to take her mind off herself....

His family's visit left Eliot feeling nearly as distraught as his wife. He was overcome with anxiety attacks, and he feared he would lose all self-control. "I really feel very shaky," he wrote to a friend, "and seem to have gone down rapidly since my family left." Finally, in late September 1921, he went to see a nerve specialist.

When his family heard of his health troubles after their departure, they blamed Vivienne. How could his creative nature survive in her presence, they wondered. Henry wrote to his mother, "I am afraid he finds it impossible to do creative work ... at home. Vivien demands a good deal of attention, and I imagine is easily offended if she does not get it well buttered with graciousness and sympathy."

In fact, Vivienne was a bit taken aback by the seriousness of her husband's emotional condition. She was accustomed to him being the strong one who took care of her when she fell apart. "Look at *my* position," she urged a friend. "I have not nearly finished my own nervous breakdown yet."

By October, Eliot's condition was so bad that he could no longer work at the bank, and he was given three months' sick leave. Unable to find an English doctor who understood his psychological problems, he went to a doctor in Lausanne. Vivienne joined him for a couple of weeks, but then she left him to follow the rest-cure his doctor had prescribed. For the next three weeks, Eliot spent his time alone, outdoors, free to pursue his own thoughts and writing. With relief, he returned to *The Waste Land*, and fueled by torment and anguish, wrote most of part three.

In *The Waste Land, Eliot* employed a new voice. Up until this time, Eliot had used a poetic persona as the narrator, a loner who looked at society from the outside, just as Eliot did himself. In *The Waste Land*, though, he used what biographer Lyndall Gordon calls the "Voices of Society" as narrator, trying to combine all of the disconnected fragments of lives into a single vision. Deeply allusive and grounded in spirituality, *The Waste Land* is ripe with images of desolation, sterility, dryness, and waste. It is a manifesto to a generation lost, a commentary on a modern society that has lost its sense of community and spiritual axis. It is a haunting sermon and disturbing reminder of the decay of Western civilization. Ultimately, *The Waste Land* declares that society is unreal.

After his three-week period of rest, Eliot went to the sanatorium in Lausanne, where his doctor saw him for half an hour each day. Dr. Vittoz would place his hand on Eliot's forehead, believing that he would be able to sense his patient's mental agitation through physical brain waves. To calm and control these waves, Dr. Vittoz recommended that Eliot concentrate on a single, simple word.

Eliot wrote the final part of *The Waste Land* as a part of this exercise. He chose to focus on the word "water," and he wrote part four in one sitting while he was at the sanatorium. Later, he said he wrote the poetry "in a trance." He believed his psychological condition had actually helped free him to a greater creativity. Describing this experience, he wrote,

> It is commonplace that some forms of illness are extremely favourable, not only to religious illumination, but to artistic and literary composition. A piece of writing, meditated without progress for months or years, may suddenly take shape and word, and in this state long passages may be produced which require little or no touch.

In January 1922, on his way home from recuperating in Lausanne, Eliot stopped in Paris to visit Ezra Pound. Pound read what he had written and advised him to cut it in half. As usual, Pound disapproved of Eliot's fascination with God, urging Eliot to cut many of the lines that contained references to faith. Influenced by his friend's disapproval, Eliot lost the new creative authority he had gained during his time away. He cut his manuscript as Pound suggestion. When he had done so, the poem lost much of the strength and hope he had found in his illness, while only the despair and repulsion remained.

Back in London, Eliot was once more sick and depressed. He met his old friend Conrad Aiken regularly for lunch and confessed to him that every night he would come home from work, sharpen his pencil, and sit down to write—and then be unable to write a word. And yet he felt he had material there, waiting in his mind. With a suicidal wife he could not console, pressured further by financial hardship and a country at war, Eliot gathered cruel, sharp impressions of London that would emerge in *The Waste Land*.

The Waste Land chronicles the approach of salvation—but it stops short before redemption and healing can be found. It hints at a deeper meaning hidden by the horror of the "Unreal," but it never quite reaches what is "Real." The sequel, the material that Eliot felt was "waiting," could not be written until Eliot had undergone a final spiritual and intellectual transformation. In the meantime, he published *The Waste Land* in his own new journal, the *Criterion*, in London, while the *Dial* published it in New York.

Eliot and his wife worked together on the *Criterion*, finding in this common pursuit at least one area of satisfaction. In fact, Vivienne did much of the journal's work. Eliot published many of her stories, finishing them for her when she was too sick to do so, but she lacked confidence in her own abilities and so she wrote under an assortment of pseudonyms: Fanny Marlow, Feiron Morris, Felise Morrison, FM, and Irene Fassett.

In one of her stories, Vivienne's characters describe Eliot's own writer's block:

> "Isn't he wonderful?" whispered Felice. "He is the most marvelous poet in the *whole world*."
>
> "He might be if he wrote anything," said Sybilla dryly.
>
> "Yes, why *doesn't* he write more?"
>
> "Because he wants to be everything at once, I expect. Perhaps the devil took him up into a high mountain and showed him all the kingdoms of the world—unfortunately for him!"

"And so, I suppose," asked Felice naggingly, "that he doesn't know which kingdom to choose?"

"He's still up on the mountain so far as I know...."

Eliot was indeed ambitious, just as his wife sensed, and perhaps this ambition was getting in the way of his creativity. He intended to use the *Criterion* as a way of getting his own work accepted in literary circles. He confided in a letter to his mother that "getting recognised in English letters is like breaking open a safe—for an American." He hoped that his work in the *Criterion* would usher him into England's literary elite.

At the same time, however, he continued to work at the bank. The long hours had begun to leave him exhausted, and he did not earn enough to pay for Vivienne's enormous doctor's bills. His literary friends—Ezra Pound and the Woolfs—tried to rescue him from his poverty by setting up funds to support him. Although Eliot accepted financial gifts from them gratefully, ultimately he turned down their offers to provide him with an ongoing income.

He knew he needed to find a way to provide for Vivienne should anything happen to him, and Lloyd's Bank was the only alternative that would ensure a pension for his widow in the event of his death. By this time, Vivienne was suffering from colitis, and she refused to consider the possibility that her husband might simply quit his job without first obtaining an equally secure position elsewhere.

Nonetheless, Eliot considered leaving the bank, and he tried to settle Vivienne in a cottage away from his own residence. Almost immediately, her colitis became worse, and within three weeks she had lost so much weight that she looked like a skeleton. Realizing how close she was to death, Eliot gave up his plan to leave the bank. Vivienne was so depressed that she threatened suicide. Eliot nursed her, while he struggled to meet her mounting medical expenses and sank into a depression of his own.

In April 1925, Vivienne's doctor had released her childhood fears of loneliness, but she still refused to let her husband out of her sight. If he did go out, he would come back to find her staging a faint. Eliot confided to Virginia Woolf that he had been cooped up in Vivienne's room for the past three months. In desperation, he penned these bitter lines:

I knew a man once did a girl in
Any man might do a girl in
Any man has to, needs to, wants to
Once in a lifetime, do a girl in.

Eliot defined Vivienne's case as a nervous rather than mental breakdown. He made this distinction, granting reasons for her collapse: her loneliness in their marriage and her fear that he would leave her. Eliot implied that it was he, if anyone, who was in need of mental treatment. Worn out, Eliot escaped by traveling to Italy in late 1925 after leaving Vivienne in a health institute. His writing during this time was full of fantasies of escape from a sexual bond. As he continued to struggle with his marital problems, he also wrestled with his religious convictions, which were growing stronger as the years passed.

CONVERSION

As Eliot grew older, he took on a new persona—the perfect Englishman. As a banker, he wore slate blue pants with black stripes and a black business coat with a bowler hat. He cultivated the proper English manner, his voice so polite and deferential that it lacked nearly any inflection at all. His friend Ezra Pound accused him of playing possum in order to escape unwanted demands from the world around him. But all the while he was wearing his mild, conventional disguise so perfectly, on the inside his imagination and conscience were in a nearly constant state of turmoil.

People who go through dramatic conversion experiences are often propelled by fear of some sort. In Eliot's case, he was afraid of many things. He feared committing himself to anyone or anything—and he feared *not* committing himself. He was terrified of his own flaws and sought constant perfection. He also feared death and the unknown. His fear and depression may have driven him emotionally toward conversion, but from his own perspective, it was a rational process. The thinking of intelligent Christian believers, he said later, "proceeds by rejection and elimination," until one finds a satisfactory answer for both the interior and external worlds.

Eliot had first visited an Anglican chapel back in 1914 when he was at Oxford, and more recently he had begun spending his lunch hours in local Anglican churches, craving the peace and quiet they offered. On one occasion he was impressed by the sight of a number of people on their knees, a position he had never observed in church before, since Unitarians were not accustomed to kneel down. Someone in his family had once remarked to a friend who joined the Episcopalian Church, "Do you kneel down in church and call yourself a miserable sinner? Neither I nor my family will ever do that!" But Eliot found himself moved by this gesture of worship.

In 1923, in the midst of his marriage's bleakest days, Eliot became friends with a fellow American, William Force Stead, who was ordained in the Church of England. Like Eliot, Stead had a wife who was emotionally disturbed, and he became Eliot's confidant in the years that followed. The Anglican priest encouraged Eliot to read the sermons of 17th-century Anglicans like John Donne and Lancelot Andrewes. These authors influenced not only Eliot's theology but his writing as well. He also turned to the Christian poets of the past, George Herbert, the 17th-century poet-priest, and Eliot's old friend, the medieval poet Dante. These authors would continue to shape Eliot's thinking and writing for the rest of his life.

By 1925, Eliot became convinced that he needed to make a drastic change in the way he lived his life; he could not continue on as he had been. He recognized that his marriage with Vivienne was doomed, and he wondered if the time had come for them to part. "Living with me has done her so much damage," he wrote to Bertrand Russell. "I find her still perpetually baffling and deceptive. She seems to me like a child of 6 with an immensely clever and precocious mind...."

Eliot could not bring himself to leave Vivienne yet, and so he looked elsewhere to bring about the change he sensed he needed. Eliot decided that combining his two worlds—poetry and business—was the answer, and he was determined to make poetry a lucrative venture. The nearly-estranged couple moved to a more fashionable neighborhood in London, and he found a new job in a publishing firm, Faber & Gwyer (later called Faber & Faber). As Eliot worked with hopeful authors, he was both kind and ruthless—gentle to them personally while he attacked their writing for the sake of improvement.

But his biggest and most important attempt to change his life was his conversion to the Anglican faith. In 1926, he visited Rome with his brother and sister-in-law, and there he set aside his constant disguises for a moment. To their astonishment, he fell on his knees before Michelangelo's *Pietà*. Later that year, he asked Stead if he would baptize him. Eliot wanted the ceremony to be done in absolute secrecy, since, he said, he hated spectacular conversions. Stead complied with his wishes, and on June 29, 1927, performed the baptism in a small village church with the doors locked. The next morning Eliot was taken to the Bishop of Oxford to be confirmed as a member of the Church of England.

Later the same year, Eliot underwent a different sort of conversion, cementing his choice to set up a permanent residence in England: he renounced his American passport and became a British citizen.

At first, Eliot's friends were puzzled by Eliot's conversion to Anglicanism. There is much evidence, however, that his conversion was not one of passionate belief, but a conversion of will. Eliot had reached the end of his philosophical rope and so turned reluctantly but determinately to the last available source of authority and meaning. His friend Virginia Woolf said of his conversion that "a corpse would seem to me more credible than he is." E.M. Forster noted that Eliot had "no trace of religious emotion. He has not got it; what he seeks is not revelation, but stability." This said more about the content of Eliot's Christianity and its importance to his cultural theory than it did about his belief itself. As stiff and prim as ever on the outside, Eliot was unable to explain to them the lifelong process that had led him to this point. Instead, like the New England preachers he had rejected, he set himself up as a prophet and preacher intent on bringing reform to a decadent society. His conversion would shape everything Eliot wrote, from poetry to drama to criticism, from that point onward.

Just after his baptism in 1927, Eliot penned the post-conversion poem, "Ash-Wednesday." The poem essentially acts out two mental "turns" prescribed for a religious conversion: a turn that looks backward to one's sins, sentencing oneself for the past, and a turn that looks forward to God and accepts His mercy. The notion of a higher world was becoming clearly visible in Eliot's writing.

Later that year, Vivienne left England for nine months while she received treatment abroad. At about the same time, while walking with Stead on a bright spring day, the two men's thoughts turned to romantic love. Eliot confessed, "I had a letter from a girl in Boston this morning whom I have not seen or heard from for years and years. It brought back something to me that I had not known for a long time." Emily Hale was now 36 years old, but she had never married, and Eliot still remembered her as a "girl."

Eliot now cast Emily in the role of Dante's Beatrice, whose being was a vision of divine reality for the medieval poet. The love Dante had for Beatrice in the thirteenth-century was a spiritual one, not based on sexual union, and Eliot turned to this concept with relief. He had never been comfortable with sexual intimacy, and his marriage to Vivienne had done nothing to help him sort out his sexual confusion. His own physical urges seemed base and polluted to him, and he resented women who possessed physical allure. After his conversion to the Anglican faith, he took a vow of chastity, further distancing himself from Vivienne while dedicating his heart to Emily.

"The recognition of the reality of Sin is a New Life," Eliot said when he described his own conversion. The conflict he experienced between sin and new life was embodied by his relationships with Emily and Vivienne. Eliot associated his own sense of sin with Vivienne, while he connected a dream of higher reality with Emily. Inspired by the tension between these two poles, he wrote some of his greatest works: "Ash-Wednesday," *Murder in the Cathedral*, *The Family Reunion*, and *Four Quartets.*

As is true for most people, Eliot's conversion was not an instant transformation. He felt as though the spiritual vision for which he longed—what he called "Reality"—was blocked by his own sense of sin and unworthiness. For him, faith was a matter of willpower; his emotions felt no different than they had before. Although he tried to shut himself off from Vivienne, she continued to tug him back into her ongoing nightmares.

The Family Reunion is a play about a man who believes he has destroyed his wife and must pay a lifelong penance in order to save his soul. This tug-of-war between past and present were at the center of Eliot's ongoing conversion. Each play and poem that he wrote described a different stage in the process.

Vivienne was Eliot's muse only so long as he shared her hell. There was no place for her in the purgatory of "Ash-Wednesday," in the sainthood of *Murder in the Cathedral*, and in the introspective ordeals of *The Family Reunion*. A new phase of religious poetry was contingent on Vivienne's dismissal. The conversion, in short, spelled her doom.

Exhausted from Vivienne's increasingly erratic and unstable behavior, Eliot decided to return to America.

His mother had died by now, so there was no one left to fully appreciate the fact that he was at last yielding to her longtime wishes. Eliot even took a professorship at Harvard, just as she had always hoped. But first, in 1932, he traveled across the country to meet Emily. When Eliot came to the West Coast, Emily was teaching at Scripps College in Claremont, California. She had been corresponding with Eliot for the past five years, and she clearly admired him. Although their relationship was apparently never a physical one, Eliot's battered heart was soothed by her affection.

Thousands of miles from Vivienne, he wrote to a friend, "For my part, I should prefer never to see her again; for hers, I do not believe that it can be good for any woman to live with a man to whom she is morally, in the larger sense, unpleasant, as well as physically indifferent. But I am quite aware of putting my own interests first." In May 1933, he wrote to his solicitor in London, requesting a Deed of Separation from Vivienne. Vivienne refused to sign it.

At the same time that Eliot struggled with the dilemma of what to do about Vivienne, he also found that it was not easy to cast off his old habit of wearing a constant disguise. A critic from Princeton remarked of Eliot, "He gives you the creeps a little at first because he is such a completely artificial, or rather, self-invented character...." When Eliot returned to London in 1934, he considered going incognito under an assumed identity. Despite his ongoing conversion experience, he was still uncomfortable being simply himself.

His relationship with Vivienne was his excuse this time for his discomfort. He was determined to not let her near him again, and so he went into hiding, keeping his address a secret as he moved from place to place in London. One drab room after another became his only home, and as a result he began to lose his own sense of self. He worried that his fear of Vivienne and the past might drive him to the point where he lost all identity and became "a spectre in its own gloom."

He found a sense of belonging by joining a group of men that included Geoffrey Faber, his employer. These men shared a passion for Sherlock Holmes and amused themselves by exchanging light verses they had composed. They gave each other nicknames (Coot, Tarantula, Whale, and Elephant), and got together to joke and talk. Unfortunately, this group did nothing to stimulate Eliot's increasingly barren creativity. Instead, he wrote crude rhymes full of obscene and adolescent humor. The role he played within his new circle of friends was yet another pretense he maintained, and he let none of them become close to him. If any of the men were so foolish as to mention in the wrong setting the silly jokes Eliot composed for their group, he would feign an icy amazement and deny that any such verses existed.

Eliot had other roles he played during this time that helped give him a sense of belonging. He spent many weekends with the Tandies in their Hampshire cottage, which allowed him to taste family life. Eliot had first met Geoffrey Tandy in a pub, but Tandy was frequently absent, off on mysterious trips he claimed were a part of his war work. He was, in fact, a womanizer who frequently abandoned his family. Eliot sympathized with Tandy's wife, and she in turn mothered him. She knit him sweaters, bought him slippers, and sent him food. He enjoyed her children as well, and when he wrote *Old Possum's Book of Practical Cats*, he dedicated it in part to the second Tandy child, Alison (nicknamed Poony). After his death, the book would become the impetus behind Andrew Lloyd Webber's Broadway masterpiece, *Cats*, the longest running show in Broadway history. Eighteen years after his death, Eliot received a posthumous Tony Award for his contributions to the score.

All the while that Eliot assumed these light and pleasant external façades, on the inside he was deeply occupied with his faith. He went to daily prayers at St. Stephen's Church, and in 1934 he became a warden of the church. In his poetry, he focused on the "pattern" of action that would bridge the distance between Time (which in his mind included sexual love and worldly ambition) and eternity, themes he would expound upon greatly in *Four Quartets*, a group of four poems, written over a series of years, which included "Burnt Norton," "East Coker," "The Dry Salvages," and "Little Gidding."

For Eliot, the "pattern" of action necessary to bridge the distance between Time and eternity had to do with failure. He studied the life of Pascal and wrote, "His despair, his disillusion are essential moments in the progress of the intellectual soul; and for the type of Pascal they are the analogue of the drought, the dark night, which is an essential stage in the progress of the Christian mystic." When Eliot spoke of the "dark night," he was referring to the writings of St. John of the Cross. This 16th-century mystic believed that the spiritual journey required a time of emptiness, when all experiences based in the physical world became meaningless. Intent on his interior conversion process, Eliot embraced this theology. He tried to empty himself so that he could be filled up with the grace of God.

Writing about this experience in *East Coker*, Eliot used language taken directly from St. John of the Cross:

> In order to arrive at what you do not know
>   You must go by a way which is the way of ignorance.
> In order to possess what you do not possess
>   You must go by the way of dispossession.
> In order to arrive at what you are not
>   You must go through the way in which you are not.

Although Emily Hale was thousands of miles away at this point in Eliot's life, she continued to play an important part in his imagination. And soon, Emily would join Eliot in England. Her coming would inspire in him a burst of new creativity.

THE WOMEN IN ELIOT'S LIFE

In 1934, Emily Hale took a year's leave of absence from her teaching position at Scripps College in California and went to England. She stayed with the Reverend and Mrs. Perkins in Gloucestershire, and Eliot was a frequent visitor.

Eliot and Emily would go for long walks together in the countryside, and on one occasion they explored the gardens of a country home called Burnt Norton. Eliot found there a sunlit sanctuary that was silent except for the voices of the birds. He experienced a moment of blissful companionship with Emily that would echo through his poetry for years. The moment was poignant, for it was filled with a sense of what might have been and never would be.

He wrote of the experience in *Burnt Norton* and then again in *The Family Reunion*, where the heroine says,

> I only looked through the little door
> When the sun was shining on the rose-garden:
> And heard in the distance tiny voices

And then a black raven flew over
And then I was only my own feet walking
Away, down a concrete corridor.

The woman's words hold the knowledge that children might have eventually been born from her union with the man in the poem; she feels the loss of this tangible fulfillment of their love. But the man is not certain he would have wanted an actual union. His words indicate that for him the phantom-like experience is enough:

And what did not happen is as true as what did happen
O my dear, and you walked through the little door
And I ran to meet you in the rose-garden.

Ultimately, Eliot was unable to have a lasting relationship with Emily Hale. She continued to wait for him, but he was far more comfortable with her as a spiritual ideal than as a woman of flesh and blood. Though he continued to express hopes for a more permanent relationship, the two were never to marry. After she returned to America, Eliot wrote to her every one or two weeks for more than 20 years. After Eliot's death, Emily Hale bequeathed over 1,000 letters from Eliot to Princeton University, where they sit untouched in a library archive; they are not to be opened until January 1, 2020.

Meanwhile, Eliot's poetry had turned to another topic— martyrdom. *Murder in the Cathedral* tells the story of Thomas à Becket, who was murdered for his faith by Henry II in the twelfth-century. Eliot identified with Becket's struggles to progress from worldliness to sainthood. The play was written for a religious audience; Eliot never expected it to have any life outside the Canterbury Festival for which it was created. Instead, it became a popular success. The play expressed Eliot's disgust at his own sinfulness. The Women of Canterbury, the play's chorus, smell "hellish" sweet scents, while they feel a pattern of "living worms" in their intestines. Their senses are swamped with hideous images—rat tails twining in the dawn, incense in the latrine, the taste of putrid flesh in a spoon. "We are soiled by a filth we cannot clean," they say, "united to supernatural vermin." A critic noted that Eliot "enjoys feeling disgust and indulges this feeling with the best of his poetry."

Pain and disgust did indeed attract Eliot. In fact, he saw them as a route to salvation. Love with Emily might have potentially been another path to his own healing and redemption, but it was a route he was afraid to take. Also, for moral reasons, he was unsure what his responsibility to Vivienne should be. He could not begin a new relationship with another woman when he was still tied, both emotionally and legally, to his wife.

Despite all his efforts to avoid her, Vivienne refused to go away. She tried repeatedly to see him while he was at work (he would slip out the back door while she waited in the reception area), and she continued to haunt his poetry even while he was determined to keep her physically at a distance. One member of the Eliot family, recognizing the strange bond Eliot had with his wife, wrote "Vivienne ruined Tom as a man, but made him as a poet." The pain of Eliot's marriage inspired some of his best work.

By this time, Vivienne appeared to be seriously unbalanced. A friend described her meeting with Vivienne:

> She gave the impression of absolute terror, of a person who's seen a hideous goblin, a goblin ghost.... Her face was all drawn and white, with wild, frightened, angry eyes. And over-intensity over nothing, you see. Supposing you were to say to her, "Oh, will you have some more cakes?" she'd say: "What's that? What do you mean? What do you say that for?" She was terrifying. At the end of an hour I was absolutely exhausted, sucked dry.

Eliot, however, believed that Vivienne was quite sane and simply worked herself into hysteria as a way to manipulate others. Some of her behavior may also have been brought on by her addiction to ether, a painkiller that had originally been prescribed for her during her many illnesses. Eliot described his sense of being haunted, his nearly murderous rage, and his guilt in the play *Sweeney Agonistes*. The play was not as successful as *Murder in the Cathedral*, since it lacked any real action. Its plot was too dependent on the characters' interior lives for most viewers to grasp.

Meanwhile, from Vivienne's perspective, Eliot had suddenly become invisible. No matter how hard she tried, she could not see him. His friends protected him as well; when she questioned them, they insisted they had not seen him. She plotted various schemes for trapping him into seeing her, and eventually, she went so far as to have an advertisement published in the *Times*: "Will T.S. Eliot please return to his home at 68 Clarence Gate Gardens which he abandoned Sept. 17th, 1932."

At last, in November 1935, a friend sent Vivienne a newspaper announcement of a talk her husband was to give at the *Sunday Times* Book Exhibition. She dressed carefully for the occasion and brought their dog Polly with her. As soon as Eliot arrived, she confronted him, her face bright with joy. He shook hands with her politely and then walked straight to the platform where he was to speak. Throughout his talk, Vivienne stared at him eagerly, nodding her head and gesturing to him as she held their dog up high for him to see. Eliot kept his cool façade intact throughout this entire display. After he was done speaking, Vivienne set Polly down, but Eliot ignored the dog while it jumped around his legs. "Will you come back to me?" Vivienne demanded, but Eliot informed her he could not talk to her then. He signed three books for her and quickly left.

Somehow, Vivienne read into this meeting a sign that things would now be fine between her and her husband. She dreamed of offering him protection so that he could write: she would give him two rooms in her apartment, with lock and key, where he could write without being interrupted; she would treat him like a grown-up son; she would leave the door open for him from 10:30 to 11:00 every night, so he could quietly and simply come home. Of course, Eliot wanted nothing to do with any of these plans.

In the summer of 1936, Vivienne pretended to go to America. She was hoping to draw people's attention to her by disappearing as her husband had when he went to the United States a few years before. She claimed that she would be visiting her in-laws, but in reality, she was desperately looking for someone who would help her cause. For some reason, she never blamed Eliot for his disappearance from her life. Instead, she was certain that a conspiracy existed to keep her husband away from her.

As the years went by, Vivienne became increasingly paranoid. Although she had been the one pursuing Eliot, she now became convinced that she was the one who was pursued. She began to fear for her life, and in 1938, the police found her wandering in the streets at 5 o'clock in the morning and arrested her. Her brother reported to Eliot that when he came to get his sister, she was "full of the most fantastic suspicions and ideas. She asked me if it was true that you had been beheaded. She says she had been in hiding from various mysterious people."

Eliot refused to become involved in his wife's situation. When her brother had her permanently committed to an insane asylum, Eliot said only that he believed it would be for her own good. Although he believed his wife to be sane, he did nothing to protest her imprisonment, and he never visited her in the asylum. She remained there for the rest of her life.

Eliot was unable to commit himself to a normal relationship with Emily Hale, but his emotions continued to be firmly attached to her. His excuse for not marrying was Vivienne. Although now he no longer needed to hide from his wife's obsessed pursuit, Eliot could not feel he was free of Vivienne. He confessed to a friend that guilt and horror haunted him daily. In *The Cocktail Party*, he wrote of a husband who becomes a "hollow man," incapable of feeling. The husband calls his wife the "angel of destruction"; "O God," he cries, "what have I done? ... Must I become after all what you would make me?" He goes on to say, "I cannot live with her," but he also "cannot live without her."

When Eliot wrote the *Four Quartets*, he expressed his hopes that he might yet find a way to return to a state of blessedness and innocence. He emulated the repetition of the Bible and its alternation of prosaic and poetic that he saw as essential to a long poem. Repetition is the very sermon of *Four Quartets*: to try again and yet again for the perfect life that was, for Eliot, unattainable. He intertwines his religious conversion and personal history with that of humanity at large in order to examine time and meaning, in some sections employing a very personal tone, as in the opening lines of "East Coker" V:

> So here I am, in the middle way, having had twenty years—
> Twenty years largely wasted, the years of *l'entre deux guerres*
> Trying to use words, and every attempt
> Is a wholly new start, and a different kind of failure
> Because one has only learnt to get the better of words
> For the thing one no longer has to say, or the way in which
> One is no longer disposed to say it.

However firm his ideas of poetry were, however, Eliot continued to harbor deep anxiety about isolation and destiny. In *The Cocktail Party*, he wrote: "What is hell? Hell is oneself, / Hell is alone, the other figures / Merely projections." Despite its bitterness and despair, *The Cocktail Party* was a remarkable success, viewed by more than a million and a half people during Eliot's lifetime. But this external achievement did nothing to resolve Eliot's inherent turmoil.

On the morning of January 23, 1947, Eliot received a phone call from his brother-in-law; Vivienne had died in the night of heart failure. "O God! O God!" was all Eliot could say. Even Vivienne's death could not free him from the guilt and pain he felt in connection with his wife. He felt no sense of relief. If anything, his guilt surrounding the death preyed on his conscience. In the years immediately after his wife's death, Eliot realized he no longer felt he was capable of sharing his life with anyone. He had told Emily Hale and his family that he wanted to marry her, but now that he was free to do so, he recognized that he had nothing to share with her. Vivienne's death shattered the long, lovely dream he had shared with Emily.

As painful as his relationship with his wife had been, it had also fueled some of his greatest poetry. On the other hand, his friendship with Emily had given his work rare glimpses of light and joy. Without these two women in his life, his poetry became flatter, less vibrant. He was left with only his feelings of guilt toward both women.

Eliot had been pretending to be a middle-aged man ever since he was in his 20's, but now his body caught up with his disguise. The same year that Vivienne died, he had two operations on his hernia and had most of his teeth extracted. His realization that he could not commit himself to a physical relationship with Emily only added to his feelings of age. He was so deep in despair that one friend suspected he had committed himself to 10 years of penitence.

He continued to be good friends with a woman—Mary Trevelyan—but he showed little emotion or interest toward her. Instead, he remained heavily guarded to those who thought they knew him best. Mary, however, was aware that Eliot frequently exchanged one mask for another. She was an outgoing, bossy woman, with a horsy face and a keen sense of humor; Eliot enjoyed her company, and depended on the practical support she gave him. (She rescued him when he accidentally set fire to his clothes and then again when he drunkenly drove into a lamp post.) Mary was in love with Eliot, but he made clear to her that he had no interest in a romantic relationship. Although she could not see into his private self, she was clear-eyed about him: she recognized that he was moody, fussy, self-obsessed, and sometimes "creepy."

Eliot would often disappear from Mary's life altogether after they had had a particularly happy time together. Eventually, he put definite limits on all his relationships, imposing formal "rules." He told Mary that it would get on his nerves to see *anyone* more than once every two weeks, and so he insisted that they limit their times together. Still, her friendship was useful to him; it kept him from feeling totally isolated from the rest of the world. Nevertheless, holding her hand occasionally was the only physical expression of his feelings he could manage.

The real man inside the façades was becoming desperately alone, despite the fact that during these years, Eliot lived with a friend, John Hayward. Hayward had muscular dystrophy; he was paralyzed from the waist down and used a wheelchair. Eliot's living arrangement with Hayward helped him remain independent. Eliot's relationship with Hayward was governed by a set of rules, just like Eliot's friendship with Mary. He visited Hayward's room once a day, in the evening, for a brief talk, and on Saturday afternoons he took Hayward for a walk. They had few friends in common, and they engaged in no social activities together. Eliot took seriously his responsibilities to his friend, but he never allowed Hayward into his mind's inner sanctum.

In the apartment they shared, Hayward spent much of his time in a room with a large window—while Eliot chose for himself two small dark rooms without any view onto the outside world. Eliot hung a large crucifix over his bed, and there he observed a set of religious rules, some of which he took from spiritual classics, while others he created himself. He memorized Bible verses, said the rosary every night, and fasted. This private life of devotion he kept hidden from everyone. His faith was a private matter not meant for public display.

Again, as he had so often in his life, he used various shields to protect his guarded heart. With Mary Trevelyan he liked to pretend to be a character called Bonsir; sometimes he even used the name when he answered the telephone. When he had to spend time in a clinic for health reasons, he often went by this pseudonym during his stay.

Mary continued to put up with Eliot's eccentricities. Two years after his wife's death, she made her feelings for him clear and proposed marriage. Her proposal was practical and sterile; a "working arrangement" was what she had in mind. Eliot answered that the thought of sharing his life with anyone again was like a "nightmare." Mary hoped that as the years passed, Eliot would become healed of the trauma he had experienced with Vivienne. Mary continued to extend to him an offer of marriage, and he continued to refuse. Each time that she pursued him more actively, he withdrew from her. He clearly, however, enjoyed her companionship and attention. She brought him rhubarb and eggs and pies, she listened to him recount the details of his days, she accompanied him to church and prayed with him, and she even vacationed with him occasionally. This was all that Eliot would grant her.

As the years went by, however, Mary began to feel impatient with Eliot. He was obsessed with his health and terrified of death. She noticed that he seemed to enjoy the times he spent in the clinic, recuperating from one ailment or another. Sickness was one more wall he used to protect his privacy, a way he could hide from people when they wanted more from him than he knew how to give. But Mary thought he wallowed in self-pity.

During the 1950s, though, Eliot's hidden mental life was once again working its way along a private course of thought. The work of Paul Tillich, a Harvard theologian, was an important part of this intense interior process. Tillich argued that self-punishment and self-humiliation will not win God's forgiveness; instead, he insisted, our only claim to forgiveness is our need for it. His theology was based on love rather than penitence, and he advised, "Do not greedily preserve your time and strength.... Keep yourselves open for the creative moment which may appear in the midst of what seemed to be waste." For Tillich, the spiritual life was one of joy and acceptance, qualities for which Eliot's lonely and miserable heart yearned.

However, his long conversion process was not over. He often remarked to Mary Trevelyan or John Hayward that he was frightened. He was frightened of phone calls, fame, travel, and above all, having to converse with a woman. Eliot froze for many years, but he harbored buried emotions waiting to be kindled. All his life, Eliot seemed to be waiting for the moment to justify and direct his devotion. When he did, he was able to let go of many of his fears. He was also able, finally, to accept a woman's love in a way that changed him completely.

A Happy Ending

At 6:15 in the morning, on January 10, 1957, Eliot married his secretary, Valerie Fletcher. Eliot was 68; Valerie was 30. His closest friends, including John Hayward and Mary Trevelyan, were amazed; Hayward had even thought of calling the police when Eliot did not come home from church at his usual time. No one was invited to the wedding, and they told their friends only after the fact.

Valerie had worked for Eliot since 1949, and she had loved him for years. She expressed her love by protecting his privacy and looking after his affairs during his illnesses, and gradually he had come to depend on her. In December 1956 they became engaged, but they kept their relationship secret. With Valerie, he could at last share his secret life. She said that she found him to be a man "made for marriage ... a natural for it, a loving creature." At the party after their honeymoon, his friends were astounded to see the way he and his wife appeared to be physically knit together. They held hands, wrapped their arms around each other, and leaned against each other's bodies, behaviors Eliot had never displayed with any other woman. A friend commented to him, "You look as if, like Dante, you'd passed into paradise." The comparison made Eliot smile.

His marriage brought many changes to his life. Love poetry now filled Eliot's works, and he withdrew from his peculiar friendships with Hayward and Mary. He paid his contribution to the apartment he had shared with Hayward for another two years, but he made it clear that the intimacy with his old friends was over. Not surprisingly, they were puzzled and hurt, first because he had never told them about his relationship with Valerie, and then because he no longer wanted them in his life. Mary wrote, "Have John [Hayward] and I known and loved the real man?"

During the years of his friendship with Hayward and Mary, Eliot had been much in the public eye. His works were famous now, and he was in great demand as a speaker at universities and libraries and even once at a baseball stadium. In 1948, he won the Nobel Prize ("for his work as a trail-blazing pioneer of modern poetry"), which made him into a literary star. Audiences listened to him in rapt silence while he spoke, his words slow and nearly toneless. His rooms were littered with congratulatory telegrams from around the world, but Eliot had hated the attention. "No-one thinks of me as a poet any more, but as a celebrity," he complained to Mary. It was "the most desperately lonely business."

Fame left Eliot with the protective urge to raise his defenses still higher. But with Valerie, for the first time Eliot felt free to let his defenses down. "Before my marriage I was getting older," he wrote. "Now I feel younger at seventy than I did at sixty.... An experience like mine makes all the more difference because of its contrast with the past." He wrote to his wife once a week, even though they were seldom separated, and he left her little messages on the Scrabble board they both enjoyed. Most surprising of all, he made clear in his poetry that he enjoyed his physical union with his wife as well. When he took her with him to the United States, he could not keep back his smiles of pride as they faced reporters and photographers. He wrote to a friend, "It is a wonderful thing to be happily married, and a very blessed state for those who are called to it, even at my age. I have a very beautiful and good and sensitive wife ... and she has everything to make me happy, and I am humbly thankful."

He began laughing more than he ever had in his life. Marriage with Valerie freed the sense of adventure and playfulness he had kept carefully under control his whole life. Until now, his readers and friends had only caught glimpses of his humorous side. They had been surprised by his lighthearted *Old Possum's Book of Practical Cats* ("Possum" was Ezra Pound's old nickname for Eliot), which contained whimsical lines like these:

... I tell you, a cat needs a name that's particular,
    A name that's peculiar, and more dignified,
Else how can he keep up his tail perpendicular,
    Or spread out his whiskers, or cherish his pride?
Of names of this kind, I can give you a quorum,
    Such as Munkustrap, Quaxo, or Coricopat,
Such as Bombalurina, or else Jellylorum—
    Names that never belong to more than one cat.
But above and beyond there's still one name left over,
    And that is the name that you never will guess;
The name that no human research can discover—
    But THE CAT HIMSELF KNOWS, and will never confess.

Secure in his faith and happy with Valerie, Eliot was freed from his old inhibitions. Now he could demonstrate the same delight and silliness he had shown briefly in *Old Possum's Book of Practical Cats*. He enjoyed jokes and laughter so much that he cultivated a friendship with Groucho Marx, the famous comedian.

Eliot had never been able to possess the quiet sunlit garden he had glimpsed with Emily Hale, but by 1963, when he returned to the image of the rose garden, he was spiritually at peace at last, and he could again claim the garden. In a poem dedicated to Valerie, he wrote:

> No peevish winter wind shall chill
> No sullen tropic sun shall wither
> The roses in the rose-garden which is ours and ours only....

Despite his happiness, Eliot's health continued to deteriorate. He was weakened by recurrent bouts of flu, bronchitis, and asthma. He and Valerie went frequently to the West Indies and Morocco to escape the cold and damp of northern winters. In December 1962, however, they could not go to the Bahamas as they had planned due to Eliot's collapse after a four-day smog settled over London. He spent the next five weeks in the hospital, while Valerie never left his side.

Eliot sensed that he was near to death, but now he was no longer afraid. "Death is not oblivion," he asserted. In spite of constant illness, his final years were filled with serenity. "This last part of my life is the best," he had written a few years earlier, "in excess of anything I could have deserved." He died of emphysema on January 4, 1965, six days before his 8th wedding anniversary.

WORKS CITED

Eliot, T.S. *The Complete Poems and Plays of T.S. Eliot*. London: Faber and Faber, 1969.

Gordon, Lyndall. *Eliot's Early Years*. London: Oxford University Press, 1977.

Kirk, Russell. *Eliot and His Age: T.S. Eliot's Imagination in the Twentieth Century*. Third ed. Peru, Illinois: Sherwood Sugden, 1988.

Spender, Stephen. *T.S. Eliot*. New York: Viking Press, 1975.

PORTIA WILLIAMS WEISKEL

On the Writings of T.S. Eliot

In the harrowing final scenes of "Apocalypse Now Redux," Special
Forces Commander Kurtz reads aloud from T.S. Eliot's "The Hollow
Men" moments before his assassination by fellow American soldier
Army Lieutenant Willard. Francis Ford Coppola's 2001 film dramatizes
the collapsing American war effort in Vietnam. Willard's perilous
assignment upriver is to find, capture, and assassinate the once highly
revered Kurtz, who is rumored to have gone mad in combat and illicitly
crossed the border to establish a monstrous and egomaniacal kingdom in
the jungles of Cambodia.

The Kurtz Willard confronts is both sinister and bizarre but he is
not quite mad nor fully a monster. Most striking are his eyes—not at all
like the vacant and cowardly eyes of the Hollow Men whom he quotes—
and his assured voice—not like their "dried ... and meaningless" voices,
either. Kurtz reads Eliot aloud with the cultured and steady rhythm of
conviction. The camera passing over Kurtz's private chambers briefly
focuses on a copy of Jesse Weston's *From Ritual to Romance* and Frazier's
Golden Bough—both influences for Eliot's "Waste Land." What a
startling image: the erudite poet, the detached and cosmopolitan T.S.
Eliot, summoned to make sense in the hinterlands of Southeast Asia.

American-born Eliot expatriated himself and became a British
citizen in 1927 at age thirty-nine. Compared with his American
contemporaries (Frost and Faulkner come to mind), Eliot put less focus
on national character than the long-term survival of Western culture and
the soul's relation to the divine. Yet Coppola gives Eliot an unforgettable

presence in this far-reaching film about American character and political purpose. "We are the Hollow Men/ We are the stuffed men/ Leaning together/ Headpiece filled with straw," repeats Kurtz, as if only these lines are adequate, only this poem suitable to carry the burden of meaning he has discovered.

"The Hollow Men" (1925) dramatizes one extremity of human experience—the psychic space between stagnation and despair—suffered by individuals and an entire culture. The poem builds on unused fragments of *The Waste Land* (1922), and its several revisions reflect Eliot's intense preoccupation with articulating the different dimensions of life and death, specifically, the deathlike states of mind in the still-living. Eliot uses images of eyes and vision to call attention to the decision we must make as a condition of living to look at, or away from, the reality before us and to understand or deny what has been seen. The inhabitants of Eliot's "hollow valley" with their "broken jaw[s]" and "deliberate disguises" have diverted their gaze from signs of eternal truth and fallen into the bleak conformity of a deadened or absent belief. Their prayers are no more useful than "[t]he supplication of a dead man's hand/ Under the twinkle of a fading star...." Paralyzed by the repetition of their hopeless speech, they suffer the additional torment of acknowledging that others—the "lost/ Violent souls"—are sufficiently alive to have "crossed/ with direct eyes to death's other kingdom."

We can imagine that Kurtz was drawn to Eliot as a companion— both daring to look at their differently but equally wasted landscapes. The riveting power of the film rises from those places Kurtz has looked upon—the sight of which has driven him to create his bizarre kingdom and accept his own assassination. Holding a tattered copy of *Time* magazine from September 11, 1967, Kurtz quotes from an article written to encourage American optimism about the war. Lies, says Kurtz, all detestable lies. With stark imagery of a kind Eliot introduced as material suitable for poetry, Kurtz recalls for Willard how he and his compatriots inoculated children in a Vietnamese village against polio only to discover later that returning Vietnamese soldiers—in a fury against "arrogant Western contamination"—hacked off the tiny inoculated arms and left them in a pile on the ground. Despite his own fury at the war's incoherence, Kurtz did not flinch from acknowledging the Vietnamese soldiers were not monsters, they were fighting with an inextinguishable conviction, which the Americans lacked utterly. He then recalls how American soldiers dropped fire on innocent people but were prevented from painting swear words on their planes. In such experiences is the origin of madness, the stuff that animates the "lost violent souls." Kurtz must have identified with the "lost violent souls." "The Hollow Men" offered the perverse comfort of conferring a clear identity, however wretched. And Coppola—knowing Eliot's capacity to give poetic rendering to the worst of human depravity and despair—called on him for poetry's mysterious power to transform experience into something not "merely" depraved and despairing.

Onetime editor of the *Partisan Review* Delmore Schwartz, writing in 1945, said of Eliot:

> When we speak of ... a new range of experience, we may think of a mountain range: some may make the vehicles [to climb up] ..., some may climb the mountains, and some may apprehend the new view.... T.S. Eliot is a culture hero in each of these three ways..... The reader of T.S. Eliot by turning the dials of his radio can hear the capitals of the world, London, Vienna, Athens, Alexandria, Jerusalem....The width and the height and the depth of modern life are exhibited in his poetry; the agony and ... horror of modern life are represented as inevitable to any human being who does not wish to deceive himself with systematic lies. (Schwartz 199)

Although disagreement about Eliot's achievement and stature is ongoing, Schwartz' characterization is widely shared. Eliot is, of course, well known for his effort to redefine, and then align himself with, a tradition of literature starting with the classical writers who had in common the capacity Schwartz cites to look penetratingly at the depths of human nature and to record faithfully both its heroic aspects and its inborn inclination for delusion and depravity. In his 1920 essay on William Blake, Eliot names this quality "honesty":

> [Blake has] the peculiarity of all great poetry found ... in Homer ... Aeschylus ... Dante ... Villon ... Shakespeare ... Montaigne and ... Spinoza. It is.... a peculiar honesty, which, in a world too frightened to be honest, is peculiarly terrifying. (*SE* 317)[1]

Eliot's protagonists struggle with spiritual insufficiency and a failure to make authentic connections with others. In the bleakest poems redemption is barely imaginable. Human gestures end in futility and disorder—"[p]aralyzed force, gesture without motion"; human speech is fragmented or absent. Human impulses toward goodness are thwarted by "the Shadow" of Original Sin and its myriad dark forces. But the condition of being hollow is not inevitable nor is going mad in the service of violent causes the only other fate. In his 1931 essay on Pascal, Eliot singles out "those who doubt, but have the mind to conceive, and the sensibility to feel, the disorder, the futility, the meaninglessness, the mystery of life and suffering ... [and] who can only find peace through a satisfaction of the whole being" (*SE* 402). These "suffering moderns," possessing Blake's "honesty" and compelled to make reflection and inquiry the most important tasks of their lives, begin to acknowledge their insufficiency—making space for the presence of God or an unnamable higher order within which the soul may begin to move away from the engulfing darkness.[2]

Among Eliot's men paradoxically stuffed and hollow is one who distinguishes himself from the "We," who in Part I of "The Hollow Men" chant together in "dried voices." He does so by acknowledging failure—"Eyes I dare not meet in dreams" and by daring to experience yearning and memory. It is not necessary for the reader to know the precise location of "There" to appreciate the sense of impoverishment implied from being self-excluded (or banished, as from Eden) from a place where a meeting of the eyes is possible. As "windows of the soul," eyes that are "[s]unlight on a broken column" may refract greater light and depth—too radiant for the forlorn soul to look into—or they may create deceptive or distracting light. Either way the speaker is aware of lost capacity, lost possibility. Figures from earlier poems—Prufrock's women idly chatting about Michelangelo; the bestial "Sweeney Erect"; and the toad-like Burbank in "Burbank with a Baedeker: Bleistein with a Cigar"—are too bloated with sensuality or distracted by trivia to be capable of any significant insight. The "I" who steps out returns to the dead and secular "cactus land," but not before confessing a failure to act and a cowardly need to hide behind "... deliberate disguises/ Rat's coat, crowskin, crossed staves/ In a field/ Behaving as the wind behaves." A scarecrow that knows itself to be a scarecrow is not quite a scarecrow.

Nor is a soul lost to violence worse than one whose "[h]eadpiece [is] filled with straw." Eliot's radical view of human nature and related necessity for a hierarchy of human values appears in his essay praising Baudelaire for disdaining the "ridiculous hocus-pocus" of his time (Satanism and black masses), instead engaging himself with "the real problem of good and evil"(*SE* 427):

> So far as we are human, what we do must be either evil or good; so far as we do evil or good, we are human; and it is better, in a paradoxical way, to do evil than to do nothing: at least, we exist. It is true to say that the glory of man is his capacity for salvation; It is also true to say that his glory is his capacity for damnation. (429)[3]

By the time of his Baudelaire essay (1930) Eliot had publicly converted to Anglo-Catholicism (1927) which establishes for the believer a clear division of allegiances: Render to Caesar what is Caesar's; render to God what is God's. When writing "The Hollow Men," however, Eliot was at a pivotal stage of spiritual development though he had no way to know this. We see here the point where Eliot's poetry—always grounded *in* the world—begins to be not always *of* the world. Or, as critic Kenneth Asher notes, elements of Christian liturgy, such as the stuttered lines of The Lord's Prayer which the defeated will cannot complete, show up as "... a jumble of shards, crying out to be reassembled...." (Asher 76–77) The stuttering voices retreat into vulnerable whimpering—pathetic or poignant, depending on one's reading, or both. Again from Asher, "[these] ... syllables of liturgy, which once bubbled up in Eliot's poetic deserts to create distant oases, ... [will] join together to make a clearly discernable promised land" (Asher 77). For now, however, there is nothing in sight except disabled souls and the wasted land.

Eliot by design incorporated the influence of other writers into his work. When Coppola's Kurtz whispers "the horror, the horror," he is echoing Joseph Conrad's "Mistah Kurtz" from *The Heart of Darkness* whose famous final words were uttered on his deathbed in the heart of a different place of darkness. There, in the African Congo, following a journey on a different jungle river to acquire ivory from the natives while "enlightening" them, Conrad's Kurtz has fallen prey to his own darkness: the discovery of an inclination to savagery to serve his greed and pride. Both Kurtzes are implicated in instances of unsurpassable human brutality and experience the fragmentation and collapse of the values that sustain human civilization. Eliot's use of Conrad in the first epigraph of "The Hollow Men" allows the darkness of a particular time and place to penetrate the universal gloom of his poem.

The second epigraph—"A penny for the Old Guy"—connects the poem to a violent event that occurred in England in 1605, three centuries earlier. Guy Fawkes, a zealous Catholic and brave conspirator engaged in a plot to destroy the Protestant monarchy of James I, was caught, and under torture gave information sufficient to dismantle the effort. To celebrate the survival of the monarchy, pennies are begged to buy fireworks at the annual observation of the event at which a straw-filled effigy of Fawkes is set on fire. Some scholars think Eliot was also remembering the compatriots of Julius Caesar whose declarations of loyalty back in 44 B.C. proved to be hollow.[4]

Eliot's conspicuous use of historical allusions to amplify his ideas reflects what German theologian Paul Tillich (1886–1965; they died in the same year) called "Ultimate Concern."[5] Tillich invented this term to describe the quality of mind that differentiates an essentially religious sensibility from one that can satisfy its yearning for life by reading the *Boston Evening Transcript* or "lay[ing] waste [its] powers" preoccupied with what Wordsworth called "getting and spending."[6] Souls burdened with Ultimate Concern are like Eliot's suffering moderns who ask "overwhelming questions." Eliot's pre-conversion years were caught up with questions about human existence that were universal and enduring. Thus we have explicit references to Guy Fawkes and Conrad's Kurtz and implicit connections to dishonorable Roman soldiers and the ruined sinners cast by Dante into his circles of Hell. Nothing essential—not time, not place, not gender, not nation—differentiates these departed souls from the hollow men or lost violent souls perennially in our midst, implicating us all.

A different manifestation of ultimate concern was developed in Eliot's early essays. In *The Sacred Wood*, which contains his major pronouncements on literature and the separate functions of poet and critic, he wrote:

> It is ... [the] business [of the critic] to see literature steadily and to see it whole; ... to see it *not* as consecrated by time, but

to see it beyond time; to see the best work of our time and the best work of twenty-five hundred years ago with the same eyes. (xvi)

In "Tradition and the Individual Talent" (1919), his best-known and instantly influential essay, Eliot connects this idea to his theory of the impersonal poetic process that sustains and carries forward the literary tradition. It is not, Eliot insists, the individual characteristics of the poet—his "prejudices" of time, place and personal emotion—that have value for us. Rather, it is in those "parts of his work ... in which the dead poets, his ancestors, assert their immortality most vigorously" (*SE* 48). Eliot is not advocating repetition or favoring the past over the present. Possessing an "historical sense" which sees "the timeless as well as ... the temporal and ... the timeless and temporal together" (49), the writer is "... compelled to write not merely with his own generation in his bones, but with a feeling that the whole of literature of Europe from Homer and [all] the literature of his own country [have] a simultaneous order" (49).

The artist's contribution to the ideal order modifies and extends the "existing monuments" which Eliot named the "Tradition." In this manner—when Coppola recalls Eliot's recollection of Conrad's Kurtz to create his own Kurtz figure—tradition is honored, altered, and replenished. Artists gain significance through their interconnection; each records a timeless quality of human nature variously manifested in history. "Tradition" introduced the first serious re-evaluation of poetry since Matthew Arnold's *Essays in Criticism* (1865) and led to Eliot's demotion of Romantic poetry. Its most radical notion is Eliot's insistence that poets surrender their individual and personal voices to a higher, more enduring order: "The progress of an artist is a continual extinction of personality." (53) The concepts of "surrender" and "self-sacrifice" are associated with religious language. Although they are used in this essay to serve an essentially secular purpose, the choice of these words effectively conveys the reverence Eliot had for literature and pointed to his coming to understand all of life in sacred, specifically Christian, terms.

No writer more vigorously asserted his immortality in Eliot's work than Dante. The visionary journey through the three kingdoms beyond death depicted in the *Divine Comedy* (c.1315) is reflected throughout

Eliot's poetry and the evolution of his thinking. Eliot's hollow men and lost violent souls bear an obvious relation to the desperate sinners imprisoned in the circles of Hell and his protagonists struggling for insight and redemption are, in effect, laboring in a Purgatorial state on earth. The luminosity in *Four Quartets* and Dante's experiences in Paradise with his beloved Beatrice share the same source.

A concentration of Dantean imagery in "The Hollow Men" appears in the lines beginning "Sightless, unless...." The alternately inaccessible and radiant eyes here recall Dante's meeting Beatrice's eyes—first by the fabled fountain in Florence; then for encouragement on the path to God; and finally as the gateway into Paradise. Abuse of the gift of eyesight brings punishment. Sinners frozen at the center of hell cannot even comfort themselves by crying because their tears freeze instantly in their eye sockets. Canto VII of the *Inferno* describes the plight of the sullen. These glum souls refused to take delight in the sweet sunshine and other earthly joys and are now consigned for eternity to a swamp where their eyes can no longer see anything and their existence is registered by bubbles rising out of the slime. Gratitude for the gift of life—that most God-pleasing of virtues—is nowhere found in the society of hollow men. The "multifoliate rose" reappears in Eliot's several rose gardens and represents Mary, the saints, Beatrice—all that is sacred. The mysteriously linked star and rose are "[t]he hope only/ of empty men." In an instance of Eliot's well-known use of ambiguity, the reader is left to wonder, is it their *only* hope? Is it *only* a hope that cannot be realized? Or is it the hope available *only* to those who have suffered emptiness, the condition for moving toward God? Only this ambiguous hope are we permitted; the reader is left not knowing what is required to make hope a reality.

Eliot famously remarked, "Dante and Shakespeare divide the modern world ...; there is no third." As if anticipating the assessments others would make of him, Eliot credited Dante with expanding the emotional range of human experience: "... Shakespeare understands a greater extent and variety of human life than Dante; but ... Dante understands deeper degrees of degradation and higher degrees of exaltation" (*SE* 252).[7] Eliot took from Dante the notion of the poet's

> obligation ... to find words for ... those feelings ... people can
> hardly ... feel, because they have no words ...; [and to

remember that a return from] beyond the frontiers of ordinary consciousness [is only possible through] a firm grasp [of ordinary] realities. (*CC* 134)

Eliot memorably gave us many words for our unarticulated experience: Prufrock "measur[ing] out [his] life with coffee spoons"; and "... time is no healer: the patient is no longer here" ("The Dry Salvages"). And Eliot's poetry is crowded with speech and vignettes from ordinary life.

Eliot's notion of the "objective correlative" conveys the poetic necessity for images capable of bearing a weight of meaning appropriate to the intensity of the emotions evoked.[8] One thinks of the scarecrow in "The Hollow Men"; the sunlight woven into the girl's hair in "La Figlia che Piange"; the "hands ... raising dingy shades ... in a thousand furnished rooms" from "Preludes II." Prominent critic F.O. Matthiessen recalls Eliot's surprise at finding Dante's verse easy to read (in the original Italian) which Eliot called a sign "... that genuine poetry can communicate before it is understood" (*SE* 238). This discovery led to the concept of an "auditory imagination," as he writes in an essay on Matthew Arnold:

> The feeling for syllable and rhythm, penetrating far below the conscious levels of thought and feeling, invigorating every word; sinking to the most primitive and forgotten, returning to the origin and bringing something back.... It ... fuses the old and obliterated and the trite, the current and the most civilized mentality. (*UPUC* 118–19)

Critic F.O. Matthiessen praises Eliot for knowing ".... before Richards and Empson began their exploration of ambiguities, that a word can carry different shades of meaning at once [depending on] the moving procession of other words.... [and for making use of the] magical properties of words [to reflect what is distinctive about a place and a time]" (Matthiessen 83–84, 86). In contrast to Edwardian poetry that diluted poetic feeling with its anticipated rhyme schemes, Eliot's experimentation with different metrical effects captured ".... the hesitation between regularity and irregularity ... a psychological perception of the precarious balance that constitutes life itself" (87).

A similar point is made differently by University of Kent professor Graham Clarke who describes his classroom preference of having students first listen to, then discuss, a difficult poem like "The Hollow Men." Clarke observes, "The very presence of [Eliot's] voice enacts ... the paradoxes, ambiguities, and gaps in meaning that are central to the experience of the poem" (Clarke 94). Listening also facilitates understanding of "Eliot's concept of the unified sensibility in which ideas are felt and sensations are perceived" (94). One consequence of listening to a poem decrying emptiness is the apprehension of an audible presence. The poem, Clarke notes, "... as much emptiness as echo, reverberates through its hollowness and gains presence as it announces absence" (95). This small (but impressive) paradox—art making life out of non-life—recalls the most spell-binding paradox of life: the miracle that there is something rather than nothing; a universe rather than no universe. (This is the phenomenon that scraggy band of St. Francis devotees went around trying to illustrate by standing on their heads to make life look completely new.) The sense of life as gift is central to all religions. It animates Dante's *Divine Comedy* even and especially in Hell where sinners are found to suffer in the same measure as they spurned God's gift of Creation and freely chose to disobey his commandments about living in it. Like Dante, who chose to leave his "dark wood" for a perilous journey toward redemption, Eliot sought a way out of the spiritual wasteland of his secular and dissolute culture. But unlike Dante whose contemporaries in 1300 considered the Afterlife to be as real as their physical world, Eliot had the special task of rendering the conditions of Hell, Purgatory, and Paradise as states of mind with meaning for bored or skeptical readers of the twentieth-century.

Douglas Bush describes the "dislocating and dehumanizing forces" influencing the modern period:

> Many of the spectres that have haunted this generation are ... the offspring of science, not merely new weapons of mass destruction but more insidious, everyday enemies of traditional order and security—the decay of religious faith and of moral values, the predominance of a purely naturalistic view of life and man, the mechanization of both external existence and the individual personality, the change from communal stability to the urban atomizing of society.... (Douglas Bush 192)

Twenty-first century readers no longer regard Darwinian perspective or revelations of Einstein and Freud as "spectres" but we are acquainted with world wars and the threat of annihilation which no generation ever gets accustomed to.[9] Bush summarizes: "... ours is a world of hollow men, emptiness within contemplating emptiness without" (193).

Even according to his own criticism, Eliot was the right poet for the time: "The essential advantage for a poet is not to have a beautiful world with which to deal: it is to be able to see beneath both beauty and ugliness; to see the boredom, and the horror, and the glory" (*UPUC* 133).

Eliot acknowledged a split in the tasks of the writer as poet and critic:

> ... while I maintain the most correct opinions in my criticism,
> I do nothing but violate them in my verse; ... I feel no shame
> in this matter.... [I]n one's prose reflections one may be
> legitimately occupied with ideals, whereas in the writing of
> verse one can only deal with actuality. (*ASG* 30)

There was no split in the person: in Eliot's famous phrase, "the man who suffers and the mind which creates" can and must co-exist. In prose, suffering is the backdrop of horror and boredom the poet must work with. In the poetry, the actuality of suffering must be accessible. It must reflect "the transitory as well as the permanent condition of the soul" (*ASG* 31).

The question of whether Eliot's use of explicitly Christian experiences impaired his poetic gift or diminished his influence created an early and sharp division in his readers. Eliot admired Shakespeare's work for having been created "by one significant, consistent, developing personality" (*SE* 203). Prominent among readers who could not say the same about Eliot was Sir Herbert Read who famously judged "The Hollow Men" to be "... the last example of what I would call his pure poetry.... All the poetry that follows, including the *Four Quartets*, is, in spite of flashes of the old fire, moralistic poetry" (Read 34).

There is a striking difference between the first lines of "Prufrock"—

> Let us go then, you and I,
> When the evening is spread out against the sky
> Like a patient etherized upon a table

and the first lines of "Ash-Wednesday"—

> Because I do not hope to turn again
> Because I do not hope
> Because I do not hope to turn

where the first voice summons the reader to a situation that could exist only in language and the second reflects on a situation that exists outside the poem. It may puzzle the reader to find the same poet writing bleakly about the failure of love in *The Waste Land* later arriving at the "heart of light" in *Four Quartets*. It is possible to accept Read's division but apply different terms—from "pure" vs. "moralistic" to "existential" vs. "redemptive" or even "aesthetic" vs. "moral."

It is clear that Eliot as a suffering modern recorded throughout his poetry a deep suffering and whatever various strategies of defense and transcendence his poetic voice could develop. Eliot suggests a unifying idea in the essay on Pascal:

> The Christian thinker ... proceeds by rejection and elimi-
> nation. He finds the world to be so and so; he finds its
> character inexplicable by any non-religious theory: among
> religions he finds Christianity ... to account most satisfactorily
> for the world and especially for the moral world within. (*SE*
> 408)

"The moral world within": the phrase implies a nature given at birth— an internal and inflexible order—that manifests its pressures whether or not we are conscious of it. He is writing specifically about Christianity but not in order to proselytize; he is describing the steps anyone needs to take to arrive at a position of belief. Although Eliot's observation followed his conversion (1927), some kind of ordering principle is embedded in his pre-conversion poetry. What causes Prufrock's sense of "failure" if "success" constituted nothing? His tortured "inadequacy"? Inadequacy to what? And what prompts him (or anyone) to ask overwhelming questions when doing so brings on intense suffering? Such is a dilemma for Eliot's critics. The reader is left to the poems—to read and reread—for this is where Eliot's struggle toward illumination and wholeness is enacted.

Eliot's poems are famously difficult with countless allusions, the appearance of incoherence or contradiction—"... to be restored, our sickness must grow worse"—or utter mystery—"Who then devised the torment? Love." (*LG* IV.2) No critic (including Eliot) insists that all allusions must be understood. Good poetry, we recall from the Dante essay, communicates before it is understood. Allusions, besides showing Eliot's roots in the tradition he carries on, illuminate connections between ancient human patterns and contemporary ones. As for incoherence—it is the stuff of modern and contemporary life. Though jarring and perplexing, Eliot's juxtapositions turn out to be purposeful. In his essay on "The Metaphysical Poets" (1921) Eliot explains his poetic method:

> ... a poet's mind is ... constantly amalgamating disparate experience; the ordinary man's experience is chaotic, irregular, fragmentary. The latter falls in love, or reads Spinoza, and these two experiences have nothing to do with each other, or with the noise of the typewriter or smell of cooking; in the mind of the poet these experiences are always forming new wholes.... poets in our civilization ... must be *difficult*. Our civilization comprehends great variety and complexity, ... The poet must become more ... comprehensive, ... allusive, ... indirect, in order to force, to dislocate if necessary, language into his meaning. (*SE* 287, 289)

Eliot's poetry is also difficult because it is about the metaphysics of belief. People commonly say they've been through "a dark night of the soul" or report an "awesome" experience. What do they mean? Eliot is trying to say just what they mean. "Difficulty" has a legitimate place and purpose; the poetry could not otherwise be authentic. Remarkably, at the same time, all the poems are about simple and recognizable human experiences: the failure of love and the grave consequences for human life not lived in right relation with divine purpose.

Eliot's poetry begins in a dispirited world where the inhabitants—including those with the luxury of cultured idleness—live frazzled and impoverished lives. Northrop Frye called it "a world without laughter, love or children" (Frye 48). Even the weather is cheerless: Eliot's people are often find themselves in the damp cold and brown winter fogs. "The

Preludes" set the forlorn urban scene: "stale smells"; "dingy shades"; "grimy scraps." A cold and "lonely cab-horse steams and stamps"—at once impatient and bored with the next routine. Eliot replaced fields of daffodils with cityscapes in English poetry. His streetwalkers encounter gritty urban details of the kind Eliot himself observed in Cambridge and London. In his chapter "The City as Via Dolorosa," critic John T. Mayer writes:

> Eliot's City is the city of the Industrial Revolution, a bifurcated city of a wealthy elite and the alienated masses, of fashionable town houses and factory slums.... Baudelaire gave Eliot his most enduring image of it as the contemporary hell, Laforgue encouraged him to write... [out of] his own experience.... For Eliot the quester, the city is the essential locale of contemporary experience: its facts of life form the landscape through which he must journey to reach meaning.... (Mayer 70)

Important themselves as parts of an inescapable landscape, these details are symbols that evoke states of the modern mind Eliot wished to dramatize. Mayer continues,

> .... it is not the physicality ... that shapes [the poet's] vision but city routines, the daily rituals that shape the lives of its people.... [T]he routines of the drawing room [are associated] with boredom and the erosion of life, but the slums reveal something worse, the misery of the masses trapped in a relentlessly mechanical daily round. (70)

In the landscape of "The Preludes," the human soul is "trampled by insistent feet/ at four or five or six o'clock." With Christianity disintegrating as the unifying cultural and ethical influence, lives become unmoored—resembling bits of discarded newspaper tossed about by "gusty showers." Eliot's sympathies suddenly engage:

> I am moved by fancies that are curled
> Around these images, and cling:
> The notion of some infinitely gentle
> Infinitely suffering thing. ("The Preludes," iv. 48–50)

Just as suddenly the voice retreats into detachment, helpless to make the world anything more than ceaseless efforts to keep warm, to physically endure like the "ancient women/ Gathering fuel in vacant lots." But the city is not a completely dead or deadening place; human suffering has been witnessed and recorded. The ancient women; the nameless person mounting the stairs to turn the key for yet another monotonous round of life; "the damp souls of housemaids"; the lives that end "not with a bang but a whimper": all these gain a stature not possible without Eliot's attention. Eliot's reserved demeanor was frequently interpreted as disdain and he endured charges of elitism, anti-Semitism, and misogyny. The reader need not judge these issues—all still disputed—but may find it helpful to approach Eliot in the perspective Mayer provides:

> Human suffering and entrapment finally engage Eliot; his own need of meaning in life, the idea of responsibility enshrined in the family code, and his inherited moral sense all urge involvement. And so the potential prophet is released in the poet, and Eliot tests a new voice, the voice crying in the desert of Metropolis. (Mayer 70)

In *Prufrock and Other Observations* (1917) Eliot dramatizes instances of modern life as spiritual death. His personae are not misfits making excuses for their failures, but souls imprisoned by a self-consciousness disconnected from responsibility and belief. In the "smoke and fog of a December afternoon" the young man in "Portrait of a Lady" (1915) sits in a pose of intimacy in the boudoir of an older woman. He deflates whatever passion might exist between them by viewing the candlelit scene she has prepared as "Juliet's tomb" and distancing himself from the music of Chopin with callow wit. When the woman speaks genuinely about music and friendship, the youth abruptly leaves to "take the air/ in a tobacco trance"—safe outside under the "public clocks." The plight of the woman becomes apparent in their April meeting when the stirring of the land (bringing the bloom of lilacs) has unearthed her frustrated longings. We hear her poignancy in the memorable phrase "my buried life" and see her imprisoned by age and social circumstance. Is she straining to look independent in his eyes by declaring herself "immeasurably at peace"? At this display of human feeling anxious about time passing, the young man smiles and "go[es] on drinking tea."

By August the older woman's voice has grown desperate—
unpleasant to him, like an out-of-tune violin—insisting their
relationship is mutual, certain that he reaches to her "across the gulf"
when clearly he does not. Fearful of this vulnerable woman, the youth
again retreats ("I take my hat") to the safety of the park where he can
"keep [his] countenance, [and] remain self-possessed." Safely distant
from the demands of real relationship, he permits a bit of song and a
scent of hyacinth to make him wonder if he is missing something in life,
but can only imagine something "other people have desired." Returning
in October to announce his departure for Europe, the man is afflicted by
a self-consciousness that mounts during their final encounter to a point
of sheer fright. Guilt, or a feeling of inadequacy—until now kept at bay
during their trysts—now threatens the man with a disturbingly real
feeling. In her presence, self-composure disintegrates; smiling is not
enough:

> I feel like one who smiles, and turning shall remark
> Suddenly, his expression in a glass.
> My self-possession gutters; we are really in the dark.
> (III. 99–101, SP)

Self-possession is destroyed by the act of observing itself. The self is a
dead end. What remains is his "music," this poem—art—created out of
detachment. But this leaves him "[d]oubtful ... [n]ot knowing what to
feel or if [he] understands." Disconnected from any human values, he is
left to wonder, "Are these ideas right or wrong? ... should I have the
right to smile?" These are satirical lines. At the same time Eliot has
made his figures interesting, more than trivial, not merely objects of
satire. They suffer without understanding; they ask important questions
their situations prevent them from answering, and they cannot rescue
themselves from the prison of their self-absorption.

The male observer and onetime lover in "La Figlia che Piange"
records another failed relationship with a woman but here the
experience has affected him so profoundly that he requires a strategy to
keep from succumbing to her again. He submits the suffering of a real
woman—a suffering to which he is not indifferent and in which he is
implicated—to his imagination which re-works the scene to keep,
powerful feelings at bay. The imperatives in the first stanza—"Stand";

"Lean"; "Weave"—show the strength of the feelings he needs to control. In the second stanza, the man-turned-artist rearranges his place in the scene—"So I would have had him leave." Images of soul leaving body "torn and bruised" suggest a sexual and spiritual violation. He seeks an easy way out—"Some way incomparably light and deft" but also confesses to an awareness of lost opportunity. Her memory troubles his sleep and his "noon's repose." Art is again not enough; detachment protects but does not satisfy.

Prufrock—Eliot's best-known figure, middle-aged with thinning hair and too self-conscious to eat a peach in public—wants his "buried life" to break out just as poignantly as the young man in "Portrait" wants fearfully to subdue his. A chronic procrastinator ("And indeed there will be time"), Prufrock longs too late for what the younger man could grasp but rejects. "The Love Song of J. Alfred Prufrock" (1917) is the first dramatization of social isolation in modern life and the consequences of repressed emotion. The epigraph from Dante's *Inferno* sendsPrufrock and the reader straight into an imaginary hell. The words are Count Guido's, whose pride is so virulent that even doomed to hell for eternity, he is still concerned about defending his reputation on earth! Critic Dominic Manganiello cites many parallels between Dante's world and Prufrock's:

> Prufrock shares ... Guido's fear of being exposed and ... need to tell his story.... [H]e can [only] confide ... [in] himself. Eliot interiorizes the encounter ... by having Prufrock engage in a 'dialogue of the mind with itself.' ... Prufrock's ... mental hell [is conveyed by sensory images] such as the opening metaphor of the evening sky as etherized patient ... which ... captures Prufrock's torpidity ..., a metaphor possibly suggested by Dante's comparison of the dead souls mired in the malaria-infested regions of Italy. (Manganiello 19)

Critic Hugh Kenner says:

> J. Alfred Prufrock is a name plus a Voice. He isn't a 'character' cut out of the rest of the universe ... equipped with a history.... Nor is he Everyman.... Everyman's mind doesn't teem with allusions to Hesiod, Hamlet, Lazarus, Falstaff, entomology,

eschatology, John the Baptist, mermaids.... "Prufrock' ... is
the name of a possible zone of consciousness ... (Kenner 40)

Critic Denis Donoghue makes a related point: Prufrock doesn't come
out of his poem. Commenting on Prufrock's observations on his way to
the evening party, Donoghue notes:

The plural nouns—'corners ... pools ... drains'—generalize
the impression and release the language from the mundane
duty of referring to something: no particular corner, pool, or
drain is intended. Cat and fog do not hold their places, as
they would if definite relation between them were in view....
The effect is to keep the reader among the words and their
internal relations, as if the apparent local meanings were an
unfortunate but necessary distraction,.... We are not allowed
to escape from the words into another place. (Donoghue 7)

Would we not, however, expect a poem about the failure of
personhood, the failure to love and connect with others, to have just this
fragmentary quality, this sense of a 'zone of consciousness' instead of a
real person? One's disconnection from underlying patterns of reality
doesn't mean these don't exist or won't manifest themselves, as Eliot
showed in "the Hollow Men." It is precisely this disconnection that
makes impossible an escape from the dead end of self-consciousness.
Not feeling "connected" diminishes the young man in "Portrait,"
"Prufrock," and, later, "Gerontion." It is the state of mind generalized in
"The Waste Land."

John Mayer notes the influence here of French philosopher Henri
Bergson, who saw the presence of two selves in each person—a
superficial "clock time" self and a fundamental self in touch with deeper
meanings and purposes. Mayer explains:

Through ... socialization ... individuals learn to conduct
themselves according to various external codes of family,
school, church, business, and ... adapt their behavior [to]
suppress their own deeper aspirations. The superficial self
takes command ... and ... move[s] unthinkingly through their
daily routines.... [A]t times this suppressed self may 'blaze up'
in revolt and assert its prerogatives. (Mayer 118)

Eliot's personae do seem to be up against something at once unknowable and unnamable, but also resilient and implacable. All fail to make some metaphysical exertion that leaves them lonely and incapacitated. Prufrock wonders, "... would it have been worth it, after all,/...To have squeezed the universe into a ball/ To roll it toward some overwhelming question," using that amazing image to represent an ultimate exertion of consciousness. But—both poignantly and ironically—he knows himself to have failed to do so—the whole passage is in the conditional. Had he done so, Prufrock seems to think he could have become like Lazarus who, returned from the dead, would be closer to understanding the purpose of individual life and death.

Eliot has created a character who does not dare to disturb the universe and whose plight arouses feelings of sympathy and scorn. It is his genius that in spite of and because of Prufrock's failures, we recognize and commit to memory many of his words.

> And I have known the eyes already, known them all—
> The eyes that fix you in a formulated phrase,
> And when I am formulated, sprawling on a pin,
> When I am pinned and wriggling on the wall ...
> ("Prufrock" 55–58)

Who does not know this self-shriveling experience? The eyes in "The Hollow Men" with their awesome power to eclipse or radiate the light of truth can also reduce a person to feeling like a trapped insect. The Boston society of "The Love Song"—a generic atmosphere Eliot called "quite uncivilized but refined beyond the point of civilization"— preoccupies itself by "... prepar[ing] a face to meet the faces that you meet." It is too late for Prufrock, not because life's mysteries become suddenly or capriciously inaccessible, but because Prufrock has been so long "preparing his face," he has become the mask.

Eliot wrote of his own terror of self-doubt, doubt about the universe, and the thought of encountering death.[10] These terrors are real for everyone at some point. Assuming "there will be time" "later" for the important life tasks is an understandable but—according to Eliot—fatal error. Critic B. Rajan observes:

> ... Lazarus and John the Baptist ... are the proper
> ambassadors of reality to the salon.... Prufrock still lives (and

fails to live) by a minor and less taxing scale of values. Visions and decisions shade off into revisions. An eternal footman holds a coat, and the confession, 'in short, I was afraid' reduces the deeper terror to everyday nervousness. (Rajan 370)

Unromantically named Prufrock wants to sing a love song, but he struggles simply to speak.

... [H]is inability to sing is not simply ironic, but part of the specifications of failure. To sing is to achieve a definition and Prufrock's fate is to fall short of definition, to bring momentous news only to thresholds.... What seems to be life is death and to die into the true life one must die away from the salon. (Rajan 369)

Prufrock doesn't sing but the mermaids do in a fantasy stimulated by a walk near the sea. Resigned to a diminished life, Prufrock enjoys the momentary company of these visionary creatures who are animated by pure and vital energies as the women chatting about Michelangelo are not. By their association with elemental and enduring forces the mermaids briefly link Prufrock to his buried life. When "human voices" intrude Prufrock awakens from his reverie only to drown in his suffocating life.[11] Cleanth Brooks concludes,

The 'Love Song of J. Alfred Prufrock' implies a judgment on a whole culture and on Prufrock as its fair representative. That he recognizes and takes responsibility for his situation keeps us from despising him but does not cancel the judgment. (Brooks 86)

"Life is very long" ("Hollow Men"); "And indeed there will be time" ("Prufrock"): Gerontion has arrived at the point in life where no time remains except that for reviewing the past and summoning the courage to face death. Eliot was writing "Gerontion" (1919) when his personal failure in marriage and career coincided with the graphic horrors of World War I to leave him in an acute period of darkness. In "The Self as World: 'Gerontion," Mayer writes,

Gerontion the individual's failure to participate in life is both a symbol and a cause of the failure of his world, that is, the world of Western culture begun by the Greeks: Gerontion (Greek for 'little old man') is the shriveled remnant of the West's twenty-five-hundred-year-old cultural heritage. (Mayer 219)

Gerontion's particular failures in the battles of his time—he was "neither at the hot gates/ Nor [did he fight] in the warm rain,"—can be generalized as public nonparticipation and retreat to private life. But he enjoys no companionship in his shabby and slightly sinister tenant house, whose other inhabitants seem to have attached themselves to the false gods of material wealth, fortune-telling, and fraudulent communion with the dead—distorted remnants of Christian prophecy and worship. The name "Fraulein von Kulp" suggests "culpability" or Original Sin. Without engagement in life (recall the essay on Baudelaire) there is no possibility of vitality or identity. Gerontion finds himself "an old man,/ A dull head among windy spaces," bereft of connection, purpose, and his senses in a "decayed house," like the hollow men whose voices are "[a]s wind in dried grass...." Commenting on this lifeless quality, the critic Ronald Bush writes:

> The poem's dominant element is not water, which has the power to dissolve rigidities of the self. It is a Dantesque cold wind that blows in the vacuum between self-consciousness and the inner life. The wind embodies a ceaseless randomness which cannot find an end and yet cannot die. (Ronald Bush 33)

To this desolate scene, Eliot brings terms of salvation. Prufrock's overwhelming question takes the form of "Christ the tiger" in whose devouring presence Gerontion must now assess himself. He ponders whether he has "not made this show purposelessly." Gerontion uses his remaining capacities—his wit and way with words—to explain, lament, and avoid responsibility for losing connection to Christ:

> I have lost my passion: why should I need keep it
> Since what is kept must be adulterated?

I have lost my sight, smell, hearing, taste, and touch:
How should I use them for your closer contact?
("Gerontion" 57–60)

In place of belief, Gerontion has looked to distracting, "cunning" history
that teaches "Neither fear nor courage [can save] us." Christ does not
comfort. As John Crowe Ransom says, "We know by now that the lamb
who came to be devoured turns into the tiger when Gerontion has
forgotten the lamb" (Ransom 151). "Christ the Tiger" clearly implies
some kind of death which Gerontion evades or is too terrified to
undergo. B. Rajan calls him "that typical Eliot character who cannot die
because he has not yet lived," then offers this helpful conclusion:

> The confrontation of reality cannot be endured; the images
> twist away into rites of expiation and anxiety, surrogates for
> the truth that will not be faced.... this failure of metaphysical
> nerve ... makes the difference between dying and dying into
> life. (Rajan 371)

What are we to make of Gerontion? We know from Eliot's earlier
protagonists the frailty and futility of self-absorption. History is no
source of final truth. The destabilizing intrusion of modern science
appears in the notion of dead as matter "whirled/ Beyond the circuit ...
/ In fractured atoms." Will his bones be reconstituted as a gull? Or is he
like the "[g]ull against the wind," leaving behind only "[w]hite feathers in
the snow"? Is Gerontion at least facing honestly his own dishonesty?
The earth for him is no final home; he feels the humiliation of his
dilemma but lacks the humility to get out of it.

In a letter made available by Bonamy Dobrée, Eliot wrote, "If
truth is always changing, then there is nothing to do but to sit down and
watch the pictures" (Dobrée 75).

Despite the appearance of "Christ the Tiger" that nearly eclipses
"Gerontion," *The Waste Land* returns us one more time to a world bereft
of unifying truth, rendered in pictures that appear disconnected,
presented in multiple languages and fragments of several centuries and
traditions. It is "... a world where prophecy has fallen to fortune-telling,
where love has hardened into the expertise of lust, where April is the
cruellest month, and where the dead are no longer buried but planted
in gardens" (Rajan 373). Here life is not possible: "... one can neither
stand nor lie nor sit."

The Waste Land turns away from the plight of self-absorbed souls to look at the wasted landscape they dwell in. Here, Eliot looks to myth for a new ordering principle amid the fragmented ruins. In a 1923 essay published in *The Dial* entitled "Ulysses, Order, and Myth," Eliot noted with appreciation Joyce's use of myth to "control ..., order, [and] give shape and significance to the immense panorama of futility and anarchy which is contemporary history" (*Dial* 480–483). Eliot also used J.G. Frazer's analysis of anthropology in *The Golden Bough* and Jessie Weston's *From Ritual to Romance* in which he found a

> recurring pattern in various myths ... [linking] the vegetation myths of the rebirth of the year, ... fertility myths of the rebirth of ... potency ..., the Christian story of the Resurrection, and the Grail Legend of purification. The common source of these myths lay in the fundamental rhythm of nature ...; [the] varying symbolism [of which] was an effort to explain the origin of life.... [and] pointed to the close union ... of the physical and spiritual, ... to the fundamental relation between the well-springs of sex and religion. (Matthiessen 18)

To overcome a poem's apparent chaos Eliot suggested allowing "image[s] to fall into [one's] memory successively without questioning the reasonableness of each at the moment ... [following] a logic of the imagination [that will produce] one intense impression...." (*PA* x).

The Waste Land (1922), drastically reduced by the American poet Ezra Pound to 434 lines, not including the novel addition of footnotes (which prominent critics like Hugh Kenner say "have bedeviled discussion for decades"), is widely read as *the* poem of the twentieth century (Kenner 150).

The emergence of new life in April from the thawing soil is bitterly unwelcome in the Waste Land because it reminds us of the need for exertion, the pull of promise and potential, and the high expectations for human life demanded by Christ's resurrection. In the Unreal City the crowd flowing to dull jobs across London Bridge— "each man [with] ... eyes [fixed] before his feet"—is kin to those unclassifiable sinners in Dante's *Inferno* whose lives were so anemic and undifferentiated that "[n]o word of them survives their living season."

About them, Eliot repeats Dante's words: "I had not thought death had undone so many."

Two memorable vignettes from "The Burial of the Dead" illustrate the contrasting interpretations generated by the poem. The first is Marie's exhilarating memory of sledding in the mountains. Is it a moment of aristocratic self-indulgence or a moment of timeless ecstasy in God's creation? Is the young man with the "hyacinth girl" speechless because his emotions are dead or because he is spellbound in a timeless and ineffable moment of beauty? He is the first of Eliot's people to look "into the heart of light" rather than the heart of darkness. These moments—whatever their import—occur fleetingly in a land of "stony rubbish" without shelter or water. Here we are invited to see "fear in a handful of dust"—a terror commensurate with a "nuclear winter" or the prospect in the dead of winter that spring might not come this year. We also randomly meet "Stetson," who, having fought at Mylae in 230 BC, reminds us of the sameness of all wars; and Madame Sosostris, who is so benighted that she warns her client against death by water—the only event in this landscape symbolically capable of bringing new life.

Eliot's views about sexuality are radical, challenging, neither fashionable nor absurd. Mainly these are enacted in the plays but in "A Game of Chess" Eliot permits us to eavesdrop on two private scenes. The estranged pair suffocating in their opulent boudoir suffer from frazzled nerves and disabling boredom. One senses that sex functions to distract or kill time, like a disembodied and calculating game of chess. A portrait of family and sexual violation—Philomel raped and brutalized by her brother-in-law King Tereus—looks down from the mantle. Hidden and silent in the painting is a hint of salvation: in Ovid's story, Philomel's suffering generates new life with the nightingale's "inviolable voice" There is no communion here—

> 'Speak to me. Why do you never speak?
> ...
> 'I never know what you are thinking'
> ("A Game of Chess" 112, 114)

and no purpose. The questions

> What shall I do now?
> ...

What shall we ever do?
(131, 134)

follow the false cheer of "O O O O that Shakespeherian Rag." (128)

In his essay on Dante Eliot denounced the idealization of romantic love: "... the love of man and woman (or for that matter of man and man) is only explained and made reasonable by the higher love, or else is simply the coupling of animals" (*SE* 244). Neither of these faceless people sees the other as more than a self-serving projection or stale partner. In the idiom of Cockney speech two women gossip about poor Lil—borne down with too many children and disfigured by bad teeth—and her husband Albert whose sexual appetite is sure to be satisfied one way or another. Exhausted, Lil chooses abortion but it damages her and destroys the fruitfulness of their union. "HURRY UP PLEASE ITS TIME": this sad scene ends because the pub is closing, but life is passing by as well.

An act of cheerless mechanical sex takes place in "The Fire Sermon"—this time between a sickly man who requires no affection to perform and a woman who eats dinner out of tins and is more interested in her appearance than she is in her perfunctory lover. Siren-like, she lures lovers by hanging underwear out the window. Tiresias, who knew sexual aberration and murder caused the pestilence that wasted Thebes, watches this sordid scene. His presence disheartens by reminding us that debased and perverse sexuality are not new, but also gives hope—remembering Oedipus—that moral outrage is possible and may again return.

What else has wasted this land? Buddha's fire sermon admonished his followers to rid themselves of the self-extinguishing passions of lust, pride, and greed. The Thames—no longer "sweet"—is a polluted landscape thoughtlessly strewn with litter and contaminated by leaking oil. Also abandoned: the departed take no responsibility, honor no commitments, "have left no addresses." The words of St. Augustine who found in Carthage a cauldron of "unholy loves" honors the perspectives of both East and West. Cleanth Brooks writes of this section,

> The moral of ... the incidents ... we have been witnessing is that there must be an asceticism—something to check the

drive of desire. The wisdom of the East and the West comes
to the same thing on this point.... the imagery ... both ... use
for lust is fire. [We witness] the sterile burning of lust.
(Brooks 157)

Death by fire is followed by "death by water"—exactly what the
voice directing the poem has been warned against. Here there is a
strange relief, a surrender to the current, detachment from the flesh and
matters of "profit and loss," and a turning to the brave discipline of right
navigation.

Understanding *The Waste Land* continues to be a task for each
reader. "After a thousand explanations," writes Richard Ellmann, "[the
poem] is no longer a puzzle ..., except for the puzzle of choosing among
the various solutions" (Ellmann 55). Eliot dismissed the idea that his
poem was written to express the "disillusionment of a generation."
Matthiessen recalls Gertrude Stein's phrase "the lost generation" to
describe those who survived the appalling destructiveness of World War
I, and writes, "There is a great difference between an understanding that
tragedy is at the heart of life, and an adolescent self-pitying of one's own
generation as being especially unfortunate" (Matthiessen 107). Eliot's
purpose was the more universal task of resuscitating an entire
civilization.

Eliot's notes guide our understanding of "What the Thunder
Said," in which a death must be (not preached but) enacted before the
(not certainty but) possibility of rebirth. Christ's crucifixion ("After the
agony in stony places/ ... and ... reverberation/ of thunder ...") and our
inability to respond to his invisible presence ("Who is the third who
always walks beside you?") leaves us like the sinners in Dante's Limbo
("We who were living are now dying ..."). Death is spiritual thirst. It
comes because there is no water, because—as in the parched lands
described in Isaiah 32:2—the cisterns of faith are empty, the wells
exhausted. We watch the devitalized consciousness approach the point of
hallucination, seeing not water, but a "[d]ead mountain mouth of carious
teeth that cannot spit" and then begin to lose consciousness with only
enough breath to faintly utter words, not sentences.

>   If there were water
> And no rock

If there were rock
And also water
And water
A spring... ("What the Thunder Said" 346–351)

Eliot's aims (and methods) were poetic, not didactic. He knew he was writing for an unbelieving world that would not find renewal in the familiar phrases of Christianity. The message comes indirectly but not less authentically in the language of the fertility rituals, the Grail legend, and Sanskrit. The voice of the thunder commands: "Datta" ("Give"); "Dayadhvam" ("Sympathize"); "Damyata" ("Control"). What do we give? "The awful daring of a moment's surrender"—acknowledgement that we cannot save ourselves; we are our own prison until we see otherwise. Human knowledge does not and cannot explain the totality of our experience of existence.

The Waste Land is a collapsed civilization, but it may more importantly represent the collapse of the illusion of a failed civilization. The voice surviving at the end of the poem would not resent the spring rains of April but neither are there gardens or trees in the landscape it occupies. Instead, perched on the boundary of earth and water, it contemplates the fragments that need to be put in order. Fishing is an activity without guarantees but it requires curiosity and hope. Hugh Kenner likens this arrival at the shore to the one made by the quester at the Chapel Perilous, who

> had only to ask the meaning of the things that were shown him. Until he has asked their meaning, they have none; after he has asked, the king's wound is healed and the waters commence again to flow. So in a civilization reduced to 'a heap of broken images' all that is requisite is sufficient curiosity; the man who asks what one or another of these fragments means ... may be the agent of regeneration. (Kenner 171)

"Ash-Wednesday" (1930) records *what it feels like* to surrender to a conversion process. Somewhere between despair and hope is an unspecified length of time when the poet—not completely defeated by suffering—chooses to stand where there is nothing to stand on. In a poem from the same period—"Animula"—Eliot makes plain his situation:

> The pain of living and the drug of dreams
> Curl up the small soul in the window seat
> Behind the *Encyclopedia Britannica*.
> ...
> Irresolute and selfish, misshapen, lame,
> Unable to fare forward or retreat, ...("Animula" 21–23, 25–26)

(Any person reading "Ash-Wednesday" will have experienced pain and bewilderment; still, it may be difficult to imagine enduring prolonged periods in the states of mind Eliot dramatizes. For relief, we can remind ourselves that Eliot also wrote poetry about cats with bewitching names like "GrowlTiger," "Skimbleshanks," "Rumpelteazer," "Macavity" [the mystery cat], and "The Rum Tum Tugger." The exasperating antics of these rapscallion cats are recorded in *Old Possum's Book of Practical Cats*, 1939.)

Ash Wednesday begins the six-week period in the Christian calendar called Lent when believers—through self-examination, self-denial, penance, and prayer—willingly enter the struggle to make themselves worthy of Christ's resurrection. About the poem Eliot said:

> Between the usual subjects of poetry and 'devotional' verse is
> a ... field still ... unexplored by modern poets—the experience
> of a man in search of God, and trying to explain to himself
> his intenser human feelings in terms of the divine goal. I have
> tried to do something of that in 'Ash Wednesday.' (qtd. in
> Gardner 29)

These "intense human feelings" include a radical honesty about the process itself. There is no sustained voice, for example, ready to join the Wise Man in "Journey of the Magi" who said that despite exhausted camels and sleazy camel-drivers, harsh weather, unfriendly towns, being called a fool, and the life-transfiguring discovery that the birth was a kind of death, that "[he] should be glad of another death."

The voice in "Ash Wednesday"—like the figure fishing on the shore in *The Waste Land*—must explore what lies on the other side of disintegration. Since there may be "nothing," the explorer must summon a heretofore unknown courage to "fare forward." The poem begins with subdued chanting, as if we are overhearing a private religious ritual; the exploration starts in each human heart—alone. The speaker knows it must transcend the cycle of hope and disappointment ("The infirm glory of the positive hour") and turn away from the world, renouncing even "the blessed face." A sense of inclusiveness and compassion—new for Eliot—is introduced: "May the judgement not be too heavy upon us." What is required? Detachment and discernment: knowing when to care and not to care. Also—that impossible mix of patience and humility—"surrender": "Teach us to sit still."

Part II enacts the "devouring" dreaded by Gerontion. Here it brings release from memory and history: the bones say, "We are glad to be scattered, we did little good to each other." A Lady appears—changing everything. As Mary, she is "[c]alm and distressed," knowing the peace that awaits believers, while suffering vicariously their pain. Presiding over the ritual devouring, she is midwife to a new consciousness. She is also a romantic image, linked with Cavalcante's courtly lady and Beatrice as bearer of God's wisdom:

> Terminate torment
> Of love unsatisfied
> The greater torment
> Of love satisfied ("Ash Wednesday" II. 35–38)

We recall Eliot's admonition in the essay on Dante about human love's perennial disenchantment: "not to expect more from *life* than it can give or more from *human* beings than they can give; to look to *death* for what life cannot give" (*SE* 275).[12]

Extraordinary effort and will are required in Part III. Mounting the circular Purgatorial stair the speaker separates from his own shape still struggling below with "[t]he deceitful face of hope and despair," resists the ease of mere aging (an old man's "drivelling" mouth), and rejects an alluring landscape falsely promising everlasting pleasure. The exhausted soul arrives at humility—"Lord, I am not worthy."

Arrayed in larkspur blue, Mary in Part IV presents a vision of Time Redeemed—a non-transmittable experience. A return to historical time—"our exile"—can now be borne.[13]

Part V records the necessary return to historical time—"Against the Word the unstilled world still whirled"—bringing awareness of the "center of the silent Word" and a compassionate God: "O my people, what have I done unto thee." Prayers are asked for those in impossible places—those who "... are terrified and cannot surrender"; "affirm before the world deny between the rocks."

Those who disparage Eliot for being abstract and detached may discover in Part VI his nostalgia for the heartbreaking beauty of Creation, for "bent golden-rod and ... lost sea smell," the "cry of quail and the whirling plover"—images from Eliot's happy childhood on the New England coast. Does the "white light" encompass these? Does the Incarnation forbid love of those things our senses make beloved? Eliot's answer is his prayer to be not separated from "Sister, Mother/ ... spirit of the river, spirit of the sea." The commandments from the Sanskrit—Datta; Dayadhvam; Damyata—become in the language of Christianity (and Dante): "Our peace is His will."[14]

Explicating poetry never improves the poetry. It is undertaken, of course, to make possible a more knowledgeable reading with underlying patterns and references connecting eons of time and diverse human experiences less likely to be missed. In this context, it makes sense to raise again the issue of Read's division of the poetry into "pure" and "moralistic," and the related "Eliot dilemma" of bringing religious, specifically Christian, material to a secular world.

Disagreeing with Read is critic John Paul Rilquelme whose book title *Harmony of Dissonances*—taken from Eliot's phrase about Donne's poetry—suggests a solution for understanding the apparent contradictions some find troubling in Eliot's poetry. Noting that "... the incongruously congruent, discordantly harmonious relations between the poems embody Eliot's version of [modernity]," Rilquelme laments that differences between *The Waste Land* and *Four Quartets* have brought about an unnecessary "disparaging of either poem at the expense of the other" (Rilquelme 2, 3). British poet Stephen Spender said Eliot knew that to survive responsibly "in times of the breakdown of civilization" one must live "not just in this time of collapse, these disrupted cities, but also in eternity, and in the city of God" (Spender 63). And author Louis Menand saw the issue as "... not different mind at work, but mind requiring itself to play by different rules" (Menand 152).

About the 'religious dilemma,' R.P. Blackmur argues that in "official" or "devotional" poetry "there enters too much the question of what ought to be felt to the denigration ... of what is actually felt.... Eliot's poetry is not devotional ..., but ... it is penetrated and animated and its significance is determined by Christian feeling, especially by the Christian doctrine of Good and Evil" (Blackmur 126). Blackmur asserts that among Eliot's contributions to his time was his imposing on us "a deep reminder of a part of our heritage which we have lost except for the stereotypes of spiritual manners" (131).

Another view comes from late author Thomas Weiskel writing about *Four Quartets* in his undergraduate thesis:

> Very rarely in the poetry does Eliot employ specifically religious terms. The function of poetry was always for Eliot the dramatizing of experience at a rare level of intensity, ... Eliot's experience was not theological but intuitive and visionary.... To abstract dogma from [these poems] would be to miss their value completely, and it is probably impossible anyway. What we can do is trace the progress of a religious exploration in the terms in which the exploration discovers experience: certainly the poetry brings us closer to the actual moments of suffering and salvation than we will ever get reading Eliot's polemical prose. That, not clarity of dogma, is the province and special advantage of poetry.

"Ash Wednesday" achieves a clear poetic statement of one of Eliot's major themes—the delineation of two orders of reality: eternal time and historical time. These two manifestations of time exist simultaneously and human life is most "real" when it is lived at their intersection. Eliot speaks with the impersonal voice of the poet in *Four Quartets*. Its purpose is to reach and dramatize awareness of this intersection. For Wordsworth, these moments brought "intimations of immortality"; for Joyce they were occasions of epiphany. In a letter to Stephen Spender in 1931 Eliot wrote that he heard in Beethoven's A minor Quartet "a sort of heavenly or at least more than human gaiety ... which one imagines might come to oneself as the fruit of reconciliation and relief after immense suffering; I should like to get something of that into verse before I die" (qtd. in Spender 54). Eliot's *Quartets* convey "a more than human gaiety" and reconfigure the mysteries of suffering from an expanded perspective that brings reconciliation and relief.

Eliot labored in his essays and lectures to encourage harmony, stability, and right action in society. Although no longer widely read or generating the vigorous dispute they once did, there remains here much that is noteworthy and relevant. In *The Idea of a Christian Society* (1939), Eliot, after describing himself as "deeply shaken by the events of September 1938," asked: "Was our society, which had always been so assured of its superiority and rectitude, so confident of its unexamined premises, assembled round anything more permanent than a congeries of banks, insurance companies and industries, and had it any beliefs more essential than a belief in compound interest and the maintenance of dividends?" (*CCIC* 50–51). For Eliot, political questions were grounded in religious ones, including reverence for the natural world and he worked with special urgency to articulate Christian ideals as the strongest foundation for an enduring and humane society.

Eliot believed drama had special usefulness for society and wrote seven plays that differently articulate the same concerns to an audience wider and more diverse than he could command for his poetry. The influence of classical Greek drama in the plays brings the ancient feelings of pity and terror into a London flat, an English country estate, and the Cathedral at Canterbury. His characters, lacking the particularity of their poetic counterparts, exist more as bearers of different (and competing) ideas and levels of awareness.

In *Murder in the Cathedral* (1935) the women of Canterbury, functioning like a Greek chorus, are "living and partly living" like the Wastelanders crossing London Bridge. Being poor, they are powerless to act, but as they participate vicariously in the growing horror and guilt surrounding the imminent murder of their archbishop, they realize that Becket preserves in his death the pre-eminence of their Church. Grateful for the triumph of God implicit in true martyrdom, they offer thanks for the "mercies of blood." The women embody the shift in awareness made possible when a momentous act suddenly intrudes on ordinary living. Becket's four Tempters cleverly challenge him but Becket resists doing "the right thing for the wrong reason" and dies exemplifying the phrase from "Ash Wednesday": "Our peace in His will."[13]

"Ridiculous the waste sad time/ Stretching before and after" ("Burnt Norton") defines the atmosphere in *The Family Reunion* (1939). Eldest son Harry returns to the family estate for the ostensibly cheerful purpose of celebrating his ailing mother's birthday, but he comes burdened with guilt about his wife's unexplained death which brings to light an unacknowledged evil in the family's history. Isolated in his suffering, Harry watches the others "... carry[ing] on as if nothing had happened." His outbursts—"What you call ... normal/ Is merely the unreal and the unimportant"—reveal a crisis more spiritual than psychological and leave the family, except prescient aunt Agatha, speechless and fearing for his sanity. The doom latent in the play manifests itself in the Eumenides whose severe mercy enables Harry to move toward redemption.

The Cocktail Party (1949) is about ways of being in the world. An estranged married couple, Edward and Lavinia Chamberlayne— ordinary in every way, not particularly loving or lovable—are reconciled through the ministrations of a "therapist" after realizing they are both culpable and "must make the best of a bad job." This choice acknowledges the desirability of effort within an acceptance of human imperfectability. Celia cannot similarly reconcile herself and chooses a path of saintly martyrdom.

Eliot has left us much to ponder. Not a didactic poet, in *Four Quarters* he wrote lines that sound like sacred instructions:

> You are not here to verify,
> Instruct yourself, or inform curiosity
> Or carry report. You are here to kneel
> Where prayer has been valid[.]
> ("Little bidding" I. 45–48)

He is speaking in the ancient chapel Little Gidding, but he reminds us also that timeless moments come as grace

> Sudden in a shaft of sunlight[.]
> ("Burnt Norton" V. 33)

As citizen in the world, living in history and seeking release from international strife, he wrote,

> ... I think, again, of this place
> And of people, not wholly commendable,
> Of no immediate kin or kindness,
> But some of peculiar genius,

United in the strife which divided them[.]
("Little bidding" III. 20–24)

His poetry astounds us:

Who then devised the torment? Love.
Love is the unfamiliar Name
Behind the hands that wove
The intolerable shirt of flame
Which human power cannot remove.
We only live, only suspire
Consumed by either fire or fire.
("Little bidding" IV. 8–14)

And counsels:

We had the experience but missed the meaning,
And approach to the meaning restores the experience
In a different form, beyond any meaning
We can assign to happiness.
("Little bidding" II. 45–48)

B. Rajan writes: "Not all of us can share Eliot's faith. But all of us can accept the poetry because nearly every line of it was written while looking into the eyes of the demon." (Rajan 381)

Eliot in company with the saints and other poets knew that life is an exploration:

Not fare well,
But fare forward, voyagers.
("The Dry Salvages" III. 46–47)

NOTES

1. For the purposes of this essay, the following abbreviations will be used for text citations: *ASG* (*After Strange Gods*); *CC* (*To Criticize the Critic and Other Essays*); *CCIC* (*Christianity and Culture: The Idea of a Christian Society and Notes Toward the Definition of Culture*); *SE* (*Selected Essays 1917–1932*); *SP* (*Selected Prose of T.S. Eliot*); *UPUC* (*The Use of Poetry and the Use of Criticism*).

2. Eliot's belief that only a few were capable of lifting themselves above

the suffocating influences of a modern culture saturated with sensuality and secularity brought charges of elitism. The plight of the "uninstructed masses" Eliot dealt with later in his explicitly social and religious criticism. He emphasized at different times a belief in the possibility of beatitude and at other times spoke of the necessity for an enlightened governing elite. These positions are not inconsistent but some scholars see here reflected issues Eliot never properly resolved.

3. Eliot finds justification for this bold statement in Romans 6.16 (KJV)—"Know ye not, that to whom ye yield yourselves servants to obey, his servants ye are to whom ye obey; whether of sin unto death, or of obedience unto righteousness"—but such grounding in orthodoxy does not of course prevent controversy or dispute. It is difficult to fit this radical view of human nature into any contemporary legal context (enlightened or otherwise), or to apply it to progressive politics, or match it with humanistic, multicultural, or self-help movements. But Eliot was less (or not at all) interested about these issues.

4. See Shakespeare's *Julius Caesar* (IV. ii. 23).

5. See Paul Tillich, *The Courage To Be*. Tillich needed an inclusive term to unite traditional Christians with those unable or unwilling to attach themselves to a formal church with those seeking meaning in the other religions of the world. Eliot's religious background combined the high passion of New England Puritanism with a preference for intellectual explanations from the Unitarian tradition. This interestingly incompatible mix generated in him an attraction to multicultural study. At Harvard (1906–1910) he studied comparative literature, the Classics, and foreign languages. As a graduate student he studied philosophy, Eastern religions, and Sanskrit. Near the time of writing *The Waste Land* he was reportedly on the verge of becoming a Buddhist. He didn't; instead, he famously converted to orthodox Christianity in 1927.

6. See William Wordsworth's poem, "The World is Too Much With Us."

7. For more information about Eliot's indebtedness to Dante see Dominic Manganiello's *T.S. Eliot and Dante*, especially the first chapter "Dante according to Eliot."

8. For Eliot's discussion of his famous term "the objective correlative," see his essay "Hamlet and His Problems," in *The Sacred Wood*, especially pp. 100–101 or *Selected Essays* (SE), p. 145.

9. For a chronology of events and discoveries that influenced Eliot's period of history, see T.S. Pearce, *T.S. Eliot*, "Historical Background," especially pp. 41–42.

10. For a rare accounting of Eliot's personal experiences of suffering, see Ronald Schuchard's "Eliot and the Horrific Moment," in *T.S. Eliot: Essays from the* Southern Review, James Olney, ed., especially pp. 191–203.

11. See Mayer, pp.127–29 for discussion of the multiple meanings of "chamber" in "The Love Song of J. Alfred Prufrock."

12. For a helpful discussion of the connection of courtly and romantic love to Eliot's poetry, see Leonard Unger, *T.S. Eliot: Moments and Patterns*,

pp. 43–68 and pp. 69–91. See also Dante's *Vita Nuova* and Charles Williams, *The Figure of Beatrice: A Study in Dante*.

13. Naming something in Eliot "non-transmittable" should not get in the way of appreciating his view that his poetry was better received by uneducated audiences than half-educated ones. He thought minds not frozen in pre-conceptions could respond more authentically to poetry's elemental meanings. For a description of teaching "Ash-Wednesday" to a random group of addicts seeking recovery, see A. D. Moody, "The Experience and the Meaning: *Ash Wednesday*."

14. For commentary on the parallel between Becket and Martin Luther King, see the "Introduction" by David R. Clark to *Twentieth Century Interpretations of Murder in the Cathedral*, 1971, pp. 9–13.

Works Cited

Alighieri, Dante. *Vita Nuova*. New York: New York Review of Books, 2002.

Asher, Kenneth. *T.S. Eliot and Ideology*. London: Cambridge University Press, 1997.

Blackmur, R.P. *Form and Value in Modern Poetry*. NY: Doubleday, 1957.

Bonamy Dobrée, "T.S. Eliot: A Personal Reminiscence," *T.S. Eliot: The Man and His Work*, ed. Allen Tate. New York: Delacorte Press, 1966.

Brooks, Cleanth "Teaching 'The Love Song of J. Alfred Prufrock.'" *Approaches to Teaching Eliot's Poetry and Plays*, ed. Jewel Speers Brooker. New York: MLA, 1988.

———. *Modern Poetry and the Tradition*. Chapel Hill: The University of North Carolina Press, 1939.

Bush, Douglas, *English Poetry*. Cambridge: Harvard University Press, 1937.

Bush, Ronald. *T.S. Eliot: A Study in Character and Style*. New York: Oxford University Press, 1983.

Clarke, Graham. "'The Hollow Men' as Exemplary Text." *Approaches to Teaching Eliot's Poetry and Plays*, ed. Jewel Spears Brooker. New York: MLA, 1988.

Coppola, Francis Ford. *Apocalypse Now Redux*. Hollywood: Miramax Films, 2001.

Donoghue, Denis. *Words Alone*. New Haven, CT: Yale University Press, 2000.

Eliot, T.S. *Prufrock and Other Observations*. London: The Egoist, Ltd., 1917.

———. *The Sacred Wood: Essays on Poetry and Criticism*. London: Methuen, 1920.

———. *The Waste Land*. New York: Boni and Liveright, 1922.

———. "Ulysses, Order, and Myth." *The Dial* LXXV, 1923.

———. "Dante." *Selected Essays 1917–1932*. New York: Harcourt, Brace & Company, 1932.

———. *The Use of Poetry and the Use of Criticism*. London: Faber and Faber, Ltd., 1933.

———. *After Strange Gods*. London: Faber and Faber, Ltd., 1934.

———. *Murder in the Cathedral*. London: Faber and Faber, Ltd., 1935.

———. *The Family Reunion*. London: Faber and Faber, Ltd., 1939.

———. *Four Quartets*. New York: Harcourt, Brace & Company, 1943.

———. *The Cocktail Party*. London: Faber and Faber, Ltd., 1950.

———. *Collected Poems* 1909–1962. London: Faber and Faber, 1963.

———. *To Criticize the Critic, and Other Writings*. London: Faber and Faber, 1965.

———. *Christianity and Culture: The Idea of Christian Society and Notes Toward the Definition of Culture*. New York: Harcourt, Brace, & World, 1949.

———. *Selected Prose of T.S. Eliot*, ed. Frank Kermode. London: Faber & Faber, 1975.

Ellmann, Richard. "The First *Waste Land*." *Eliot in His Time: Essays on the Occasion of the Fiftieth Anniversary of* The Waste Land. Princeton: Princeton University Press, 1973.

Frye, Northrup. *T.S. Eliot*. New York: Capricorn Books, 1963.

Gardner, Helen. *The Composition of the* Four Quartets. New York: Oxford University Press, 1978.

Clarke, David R., ed. *Twentieth Century Interpretations of Murder in the Cathedral*. Upper Saddle River, NJ: Prentice Hall, 1971.

Conrad, Joseph. *The Collected Works of Joseph Conrad*. London: Heinemann, 1921.

Herbert Read, "T.S.E.—A Memoir." *T.S. Eliot: The Man and His Work*, ed. Allen Tate. New York: Delacorte Press, 1966.

Kenner, Hugh. *The Invisible Poet: T.S. Eliot*. London: W.H. Allen, 1960.

Manganiello, Dominic. *T.S. Eliot and Dante*. New York: St. Martin's Press, 1989.

Mattheissen, F.O. *The Achievement of T.S. Eliot: An Essay on the Nature of Poetry*. Oxford: Oxford University Press, 1958.

Mayer, John T. *T.S. Eliot's Silent Voices*. Oxford: Oxford University Press, 1989.

Menand, Louis. *Discovering Modernism: T.S. Eliot and His Context*. Oxford: Oxford University Press, 1989.

Moody, A.D. "The Experience and the Meaning: *Ash-Wednesday*." *Approaches to Teaching Eliot's Poetry and Plays*, ed. Jewel Spears Brooker. New York: MLA, 1988.

Pearce, T.S. *T.S. Eliot*. New York: Arco Publishing Company, 1989.

Rajan, B. *The Overwhelming Question: A Study of the Poetry of T S. Eliot*. Toronto: University of Toronto Press, 1976.

Ransom, John Crowe "Gerontion." *T.S. Eliot: The Man and His Work*, ed. Allen Tate. New York: Delacorte Press, 1966.

Riquelme, John Paul. *The Harmony of Dissonance*. Baltimore: Johns Hopkins University Press, 1991.

Schuchard, Ronald. "Eliot and the Horrific Moment." *T.S. Eliot:Essays from the Southern Review*, ed. James Olney. Oxford: Clarendon Press, 1988.

Schwartz, Delmore. "T.S. Eliot as the International Hero." *Partisan Review*, Spring 1945.

Spender, Stephen "Remembering Eliot." *T.S. Eliot: The Man and His Work*, ed. Allen Tate. New York: Delacorte Press, 1966.

Tillich, Paul. *The Courage to Be*. New Haven: Yale University Press, 1952.

Unger, Leonard. *T.S. Eliot, Moments and Patterns*. Minneapolis: University of Minnesota Press, 1966.

Williams, Charles. *The Figure of Beatrice*. London: Faber & Faber, Ltd., 1943.

F.O. MATTHIESSEN

The 'Objective Correlative'

> What is *not* interesting, is that which does not add to our knowledge
> of any kind; that which is vaguely conceived and loosely drawn; a
> representation which is general, indeterminate, and faint, instead of
> being particular, precise, and firm... What are the eternal objects of
> poetry, among all nations and at all times? They are actions; human
> actions.
>
> —Matthew Arnold, Preface to *Poems*, 1853

If the natural demands of their mediums took Joyce and Eliot to the
opposite poles of expansion and compression, the qualities of experience
they were endeavouring to present were enough alike to lead to marked
parallels in certain of their qualities of expression. As Eliot observed in
an unpublished lecture on the method of Ulysses (1933): 'In some minds
certain memories, both from reading and life, become charged with
emotional significance. All these are used, so that intensity is gained at
the expense of clarity.' There could not be a closer annotation of Eliot's
own method, and I therefore want to consider some of its implications.
It is no longer necessary, as it would have been, before the lyrical impulse
of his poetry had been generally perceived, to spend much time
defending Eliot's work against the charge of being over-intellectualized.
He has himself taken pains on many occasions to point out that the
concern of the poet is never with thought so much as with finding 'the

---

From *The Achievement of T.S. Eliot: An Essay on the Nature of Poetry* © 1947 by Oxford
University Press. Reprinted by permission.

emotional equivalent of thought'; that the essential function of poetry is not intellectual but emotional; that the business of Dante or Shakespeare was 'to express the greatest emotional intensity of his time, based on whatever his time happened to think.' All that he insists is that the more intelligent the poet is the better, since he is thus likely to be wider in his interests and more mature in his expression of them. He believes also that 'fundamental brain-work' can be justly demanded of the reader, particularly since 'our civilization, as it exists at present ... comprehends great variety and complexity, and this variety and complexity, playing upon a refined sensibility, must produce various and complex results.' But purely in terms of the elements of tradition which Eliot has attempted to bring to fresh expression in his own poetry, it is by now apparent that his principal desire is not for intellectual density but for richness and subtlety of emotional impression.

But in his effort to convey the full intricacy of the moment, in his own partial sacrifice of clarity for range of implication, it is perhaps still necessary to show that he is not making obscure or arbitrary associations which are too personal to be followed by the reader. Actually Eliot was not being in the least paradoxical when he stressed the importance to the poet of Dante's power to create 'clear, visual images.' For he has repeatedly insisted that 'the poet does not aim to excite—that is not even a test of his success—but to set something down.' What he means by that is the prime importance of concrete presentation of carefully observed details. (It should not be forgotten that the title of his first book was *Prufrock and Other Observations*.) He is therein close to Hulme's conviction that 'the great aim is accurate, precise, and definite description,'[1] close to Ezra Pound's preoccupation in finding the exact fresh word, related also to the sharp visual discoveries of modern painting from Cézanne to Picasso. Eliot compresses his descriptions so tightly that you have to give them time to unfold in your mind:

> The river's tent is broken: the last fingers of leaf
> Clutch and sink into the wet bank. The wind
> Crosses the brown land, unheard.

It takes many readings of 'The Fire Sermon' before you see how complete a picture of the river's desolation is revealed to you from the moment of those opening three lines: the tearing away of the lovely ampleness with which summer trees form a canopy over the stream, leaving the bleak bareness of autumn; the sinister undertone that is started by seeing the leaves as drowning fingers clutching at the bank; the utter desertion conveyed by the fact that the wind is unheard. It is as true of these lines as Eliot found it of Coleridge's imagery stored-up from the voyagers that 'it is usually the accurate images, the fidelity of which may still be recognized, that are the most telling.'

To be sure, Eliot's observations are not primarily of physical objects; his most sustained analysis is applied to states of mind and emotion. But he holds none the less that permanent poetry is always a presentation of thought and feeling 'by a statement of events in human action or objects in the external world.' In his view the poet's emotions are not *in themselves* important; as he remarked in elucidation of Valéry, 'not our feelings, but the pattern which we make of our feelings is the centre of value.' The lasting poem is not the result of pouring out personal emotion, for 'the only way of expressing emotion in the form of art is by finding an "objective correlative"; in other words, a set of objects, a situation, a chain of events which shall be the formula of that *particular* emotion; such that when the external facts, which must terminate in sensory experience are given, the emotion is immediately evoked.' This passage will not yield its full significance without careful reading; but it is already a *locus classicus* of criticism.[2] It furnishes, for example, the exact clue to the triumph of *Samson Agonistes*, to Milton's complete success there in finding a dramatic situation that would externalize his own emotions and thus give them universal stature. On the other hand, failure to find an adequate 'chain of events,' and a consequent confusion of purely personal feelings with those of the hero is what leaves Shelley's *Prometheus Unbound* so vague and vaporous. And the reason why 'Gerontion' is the most mature, balanced work of art among Eliot's earlier poems is that he hit upon a situation in the sombre brooding of the old man that enabled him to set down a particular statement of life in concrete objectified form.

He is not writing in his own person:[3] the situation of Gerontion is even farther from his own than that of the middle-aged Prufrock had been when Eliot created him while still in his early twenties. I do not mean that elements of Eliot's own experience, of his own thought and feeling, do not enter into these characters; in fact, the source of some of the wittiest irony in 'Prufrock' would seem to spring from Eliot's detached ability to mock also the supercultivated fastidious young man from Harvard. But the point is that the hero of the poem is not such a figure; and that, as a result, Eliot's rapier thrusts have full play with no risk of becoming clumsily involved in purely personal associations. By choosing a character apart from his immediate experience he has been able to concentrate entirely, not on his own feelings, but on the creation of his poem. Thus everything important which he had to say about a certain kind of frustration and longing also found its articulation in this objectified transmuted form; just as the double feeling of his repulsion from vulgarity, and yet his shy attraction to the coarse earthiness of common life have found their complete symbol in Sweeney. And so, in like fashion, Eliot can project into the thoughts of Gerontion an expression of one of his most moving, recurrent themes: the horror of a life without faith, its disillusioned weariness of knowledge, its agonized slow drying up of the springs of emotion.

It should now also be clear that his understanding of the value of the 'objective correlative' was what caused Eliot to base the dramatic lyric intensity of *The Waste Land* in the externalized structure of parallel myths. It also led him to give the poem even further focus by sifting it through the eyes of a central observer, Tiresias—a device which Eliot may have learned in part from Henry James's similar use of Strether in *The Ambassadors*. As Eliot states in a note, 'What Tiresias *sees*, in fact, is the substance of the poem.' And Tiresias is the exact symbol for such haunting inclusive consciousness: only Tiresias, who had experienced life both as a man and a woman, who, though blind, possessed the torturing faculty of being able to foresee the future, could contain in his vision the ranges of life in a great metropolis. Only his infinitely sensitive power to 'foresuffer all' could embrace the violent contrasts (and samenesses) that are now packed into the compass of a few square blocks: the dead luxury of the upper class, the vast uninspired bourgeois existence, the broken fragments of the talk of the poor overheard in a bar. Incidentally, the clearest perception of Eliot's range in ability to fit his style to his subject is furnished by the remarkably different manners in which he presents these three classes of society. Perhaps the sharpest dramatic effect in the whole poem lies in the contrasting halves of 'The Game of Chess,' the abrupt shift from an elaborately sensuous style that can build up an atmosphere of cloying richness to one which catches the very cadences of Cockney speech in a pub. And then, in the next section, in order to suggest the huge commercialized world that lies between *these two* extremes, Eliot portrays the characteristic scene between the typist and the clerk, and suggests the denatured quality of their life by a deliberate mechanization of his rhythm, as well as by the first continuous use of rhyme in the poem, which, being unexpected, contributes to heighten his effect. At the same time, beneath all these contrasts in appearance, are being stressed the similar human situations in which all these different people are found: they are all playing the same stale game, burning alike with sterile desire. They stand in common need of regeneration.

Eliot's steady emphasis on the importance of wholeness of construction perhaps explains best why it is fair to separate Pound and Eliot by saying that 'Pound avait étudié la diction poétique, Eliot étudie le style.'[4] This distinction is not intended in the least to minimize Eliot's very great obligations to Pound, or the stimulus which he received from the slightly elder poet's first enunciation of his poetic theory in the years when Eliot was just out of college. Pound dwelt on the necessity of distinct presentation of something concrete; on accuracy and economy of language—'to use absolutely no word that does not contribute to the presentation'; and, regarding rhythm, on the necessity of composing 'in the sequence of the musical phrase, not in the sequence of the metronome.'[5] That Eliot has followed all three of these technical principles is to be seen everywhere in his work.

Pound also defined the nature of an image in such a way as to stress the union of sense and thought, the presence of the idea in the image: 'An "Image" is that which presents an intellectual and emotional complex in an instant of time.' That definition would seem to be in the direction of the 'objective correlative,' and would certainly apply directly to what Eliot was trying to do, for instance, in such a line as

I have measured out my life with coffee spoons.

But the trouble is that Pound virtually stopped short with the definition of details; and it remained for Eliot to bring such technical discoveries to their full fruition by building them into an architectural whole. This limitation of Pound's may help to explain why his greatest success has been in his translations, where he had an external structure to rely upon and could give his entire care to his extraordinary verbal and rhythmical expertness; as well as why his *Cantos*, though they have already proved a school of versification for younger poets, are comparatively formless; and why his most living original poems are the *Hugh Selwyn Mauberley* series of 1920, which show how Pound, in his turn, had begun to feel the influence of the method of Eliot.

A passage from 'Gerontion' will furnish perhaps the best example of the kind of hard precision with which Eliot's reliance upon 'a set of objects' enables him to thread together the range of his associations:

> I an old man,
> A dull head among windy spaces.
>
> Signs are taken for wonders. 'We would see a sign!'
> The word within a word, unable to speak a word,
> Swaddled with darkness. In the juvescence of the year
> Came Christ the tiger
>
> In depraved May, dogwood and chestnut, flowering judas,
> To be eaten, to be divided, to be drunk
> Among whispers; by Mr. Silvero
> With caressing hands, at Limoges
> Who walked all night in the next room;
>
> By Hakagawa, bowing among the Titians;
> By Madame de Tornquist, in the dark room
> Shifting the candles; Fraülein von Kulp
> Who turned in the hall, one hand on the door.
>   Vacant shuttles
> Weave the wind. I have no ghosts,
> An old man in a draughty house
> Under a windy knob.

The transitions are sudden, but, in terms of the context, unmistakable. There could hardly be a more effective way of stressing the intimate connection between the mysteries of religion and sex than by linking together the Christian story with the upsurging energies of spring. Yet it is also 'depraved' May, and suddenly we are aware that it is not just the Holy Communion that is being eaten and drunk 'among whispers': that last phrase also relates to the empty, slightly sinister cosmopolitan world in which Gerontion's life has been betrayed, his passion and ardour have been divided and lost.[6] The series of glimpses of various figures in this world illustrates what Eliot tries to convey by his use of images. His design is to give the *exact* perceived detail, without comment, and let that picture carry its own connotations. As he said once in conversation, the images here are 'consciously concrete'; they correspond as closely as possible to something he has actually seen and remembered. But he also believes that if they are clearly rendered, they will stand for something larger than themselves; they will not depend for their apprehension upon any private reference, but will become 'unconsciously general.'

A similar example of his use of imagery is provided by a passage in the final poem of *Ash Wednesday*, which is also notable in revealing the direction in which Eliot had travelled in the ten years intervening since 'Gerontion.' His technique is greatly simplified: the quick contrasts of Donne and Laforgue have been replaced by something nearer to the limpidity of Dante. He wants to embody the reflection that although he desires to focus his mind upon God, although his spirit, in its ascent of the purgatorial mount, does not want to be distracted any longer by sensuous beauty, still,

> though I do not wish to wish these things,
> From the wide window towards the granite shore
> The white sails still fly seaward, seaward flying
> Unbroken wings
>
> And the lost heart stiffens and rejoices
> In the lost lilac and the lost sea voices
> And the weak spirit quickens to rebel
> For the bent golden-rod, and the lost sea smell
> Quickens to recover
> The cry of quail and the whirling plover
> And the blind eye creates
> The empty forms between the ivory gates
> And smell renews the salt savor of the sandy earth

It is impossible to divorce the reflection from the imagery. Exact description of memories of the varied loveliness of the New England coast expresses the very sensation of his distraction, of his turning, in spite of his will, away from the contemplation of God. He is momentarily forgetful of the penance of humility appointed for Ash Wednesday; for he has been lured back to the human realm of desire and loss by the enchantment of the senses.

I do not want to give the impression of trying to make Eliot's poetry seem easy, or of trying to demonstrate that his lines possess just one restricted meaning. Indeed, by his own account of the 'consciously concrete' and 'unconsciously general,' it is apparent that he believes that poetry should suggest much more than it can state directly to the mind. However, recognition of this impalpable element in poetry, of the fact that its range of meaning inevitably varies for different readers, does not diminish in the least the poet's responsibility to centre on the specific and distinct. Eliot notes that speaking of 'the incommunicable' in literature may often mean merely 'the vague and unformed.' His understanding of the fact that 'suggestion' is of doubtful worth unless radiating from a solid core of meaning, lies behind his analysis of why a confessedly slight poem like Marvell's 'The Nymph and the Fawn' is so much more satisfactory than William Morris's comparable effort in 'The Nymph's Song to Hylas':

> The effect of Morris's charming poem depends upon the mistiness of the feeling and the vagueness of its object; the effect of Marvell's poem upon its bright, hard precision ... The verses of Morris, which are nothing if not an attempt to suggest, really suggest nothing; and we are inclined to infer that the suggestiveness is the aura around a bright clear centre, that you cannot have the aura alone.

This necessity to concentrate on something definite is exactly what Eliot means by his repeated statement that the evocation of emotion by means of complete, concrete objectification is the only right way of expressing emotion in art. The way in which Eliot secures both definiteness of statement and indefiniteness of suggestion by building his imagery upon an objective structure can be seen in the third poem in *Ash Wednesday*:

> At the first turning of the second stair
> I turned and saw below

The same shape twisted on the banister
Under the vapour in the fetid air
Struggling with the devil of the stairs who wears
The deceitful face of hope and of despair.

At the second turning of the second stair
I left them twisting, turning below;
There were no more faces and the stair was dark,
Damp, jaggèd, like an old man's mouth drivelling,
                    beyond repair,
Or the toothed gullet of an agèd shark.

At the first turning of the third stair
Was a slotted window bellied like the fig's fruit
And beyond the hawthorn blossom and a pasture scene
The broadbacked figure drest in blue and green
Enchanted the maytime with an antique flute.
Blown hair is sweet, brown hair over the mouth blown,
Lilac and brown hair;
Distraction, music of the flute, stops and steps of the mind
            over the third stair,
Fading, fading; strength beyond hope and despair
Climbing the third stair.

Lord, I am not worthy
Lord, I am not worthy

        but speak the word only.

The symbol of the stair is perfectly concrete whether or not we identify
it with Dante's purgatorial mount. For, in either case, the rhythms give
us the feeling of difficult climbing movement; and each turning of the
stair presents a distinct stage of spiritual struggle. The sinister horror of
what he saw below him at the first turning is heightened by the very
ambiguousness of the expression, 'the same shape.' Does it mean a
spectre that he has been fleeing from and has felt to be pursuing him up
the stair? Or, more terrifying still, does it mean his own very likeness,
thus stressing the obsession with self, the inability of the individual to

escape from the bonds of his own identity? Such thoughts constituted one of the principal torments for the poet of *The Waste Land*, who had

> heard the key
> Turn in the door once and turn once only,

who was unable to break through the circle of his own loneliness by giving himself up to any belief, and so, with nothing external or absolute to base his life upon, felt himself mocked equally by hope and despair, since both were equally groundless. In keeping with such reflections, the damp blackness of the second turning could represent the state of mind voiced in 'The Hollow Men,' although, speaking strictly, the utter emptiness which pervades that poem would seem to belong more entirely to an *Inferno*. But with the next turning, the poet has moved on to a third state, forgetting his despair in a glimpse of the loveliness possible in this world, and yet looking now to something 'beyond hope and despair,' to faith which shall sustain him, to his salvation through divine grace.

In such a manner Eliot's images are at the same time both exact and suggestive in their portrayal of these three spiritual stages. It is more than likely that he meant the turnings of his stair to represent something even more definite, to remind the reader that they correspond in general to the three main divisions of Dante's hill of Purgatory.[7] At the foot of the hill were those whose sin had been the greatest, who had been guilty of love distorted, those who had loved evil things instead of God, those whose self-absorbed pride had shut them off from Him. Higher up were those whose love of God had been defective; higher still, the least gravely sinful, those who had loved excessively things which should take only a secondary place in the affections, among them the sensual and lustful. (A hint of the correspondence between these particular qualities of excess and Eliot's third stair is underscored by the image describing the window itself 'bellied like the fig's fruit.') Such a reminder that the stages of the soul which Eliot is depicting correspond also to a completely developed pattern of philosophic and religious thought, would remove the experience from anything purely personal, and would thus enable it to possess a more universal significance.

Perhaps the most important thing that is revealed by applying Eliot's conception of the 'objective correlative' to his own work is the essentially dramatic nature of all his poetry. What is said by one of the speakers in his 'Dialogue on Dramatic Poetry' certainly seems expressive of one of his own most sustained beliefs:

> What great poetry is not dramatic? Even the minor writers of the Greek Anthology, even Martial, are dramatic. Who is more dramatic than Homer or Dante? We are human beings, and in what are we more interested than in human action and human attitudes? Even when he assaults, and with supreme mastery, the divine mystery, does not Dante engage us in the question of the human attitude towards this mystery—which is dramatic?

In the terms of this description the dramatic element in poetry lies in its power to communicate a sense of real life, a sense of *the immediate present*—that is, of the full quality of a moment as it is actually felt to consist. It was Ezra Pound's great service to modern poetry to rescue the lyric from musical prettiness by his reaffirmation of the importance of such direct presentation of actuality, by his determination, as he declared in his manifesto 'Against the Crepuscular Spirit in Modern Poetry,' to substitute 'for dreams—men.'[8] This ability to portray the very character of life is rare since it depends upon a firm grasp of experience, and thus demands from the poet a unified sensibility, a capacity of feeling that can closely interweave emotion and thought. It likewise demands a mature realization of the existence of both good and evil, an understanding that life takes on dramatic significance only when perceived as a struggle between these forces. Thus, despite Pound's emphasis on 'human action,' his failure to distinguish between individual responsibility for evil and social circumstance has the result of making his journalistic conception of Hell in the *Cantos* utterly lacking in tragic dignity—a Hell, as Eliot has remarked, 'for the *other people*, the people we read about in the newspapers, not for oneself and one's friends.' Such a Hell not only robs any implied Heaven of all authenticity, but also inevitably renders much of Pound's observation of human beings 'trivial and accidental.'

In the light of these reflections it becomes apparent that the ability to convey a sense of human reality is also destroyed by any facile idealization, or by any effort to escape into a dream world through the hypnosis of sound. The dramatic quality is also wholly lost by the merely reflective poet who, instead of making a union of emotion and thought, instead of thinking in images and thus bringing a living body to his ideas, tends to put his images aside and to fall back on abstract rhetoric when he comes to deliver his statements:

> We look before and after
>> And pine for what is not:
> Our sincerest laughter
>> With some pain is fraught;
> Our sweetest songs are those that tell of saddest thought.[9]

These reflections perhaps also make clear why it is accurate to say that Donne is a dramatic poet but not Spenser; that the songs of Campion and Shakespeare are dramatic but not those of Swinburne,[10] or why Keats at the time of his death was increasingly absorbed with the desire to write plays;[11] or why, among poets of seemingly equal stature like Wyatt and Surrey, the ability to cut through graceful Renaissance decoration of sentiment to a bare statement of immediate emotion is what gives a few poems of the former their heightened vitality.[12]

In defining Eliot's particular dramatic quality it is relevant to quote Rémy de Gourmont's brief characterization of symbolism, in his *Book of Masks*: 'a tendency to take only the characteristic detail out of life, to pay attention only to the act by which a man distinguishes himself from another man, and to desire only to realize essentials, results.' There could hardly be a better account of the way in which Eliot endeavours to portray 'human action and human attitudes.' He sets out to make his characters actual by confining his description of them to a perceived significant detail or characteristic gesture. This is the method by which he lets us conceive the nature of Princess Volupine by means of a glimpse of her outstretched 'meagre, blue-nailed, phthisic hand.' Or again, he creates the dramatic relevance of the figures who throng Gerontion's memory by the way he shows each of them in action. He wants to intermingle description and event in the manner in which they actually associate in a person's impressions; this is the intention emphasized by his statement that he was stimulated by Henry James' example in *The Aspern Papers* to try 'to make a place real not descriptively but by something happening there.' What 'happens' in Eliot's shorter poems is frequently no more than a single observed impression: a girl standing at the top of a stairway 'with a fugitive resentment' in her eyes; a young man handing his cousin the evening paper. Yet, as also in James, there is something both pictorial and dramatic in this single impression, something acutely revelatory of the people described. As James remarked in 'The Art of Fiction':

> What is a picture or a novel that is *not* of character? What else do we seek in it and find in it? It is an incident for a woman to stand up with her hand resting on a table and look out at you in a certain way; or if it be not an incident, I think it will be hard to say what it is. At the same time it is an expression of character.

These sentences might describe the effect of Eliot's 'La Figlia che Piange' equally as well as that of one of James's own stories. The more one thinks of Eliot in relation to James, the more one realizes the extent of the similarities between them. They are similarities of content as well as of method. Both James and Eliot, no less than Hawthorne, are mainly concerned with what lies behind action and beneath appearance. In their effort to find the exact situation that will evoke an impression of the inner life, they are occupied too in expressing like states of mind and feeling. Prufrock's rankling inability to give himself to life and the kind of frustration embodied in Eliot's 'Portrait of a Lady' find their parallels many times in James. But even more significant is the realization that the qualities of spirit that rise above frustration in Eliot's later poems, as well as in James's *Portrait of a Lady* or *The Wings of the Dove*, are those which affirm the value of renunciation, sympathy, and tenderness. These qualities have long been dominant in the American strain. All three are to be found in Emily Dickinson, if with a somewhat different effect than in Hawthorne; and the two last are Whitman's most enduring tones in 'When lilacs last in the dooryard bloomed.'

NOTES

1. Hulme was killed in action in 1917, and his essays on 'Humanism and the Religious Attitude,' 'Modern Art and Philosophy,' and 'Romanticism and Classicism,' written just before the First World War, were not published until 1924, under the general title of *Speculations*. Eliot had not known Hulme

personally, though he had heard much about him from Pound; and he had not read any of Hulme's essays before they were published, by which time Eliot's own theory of poetry had already matured. Nevertheless certain sentences, from 'Romanticism and Classicism' in particular, foreshadow so exactly a number of the principles which Eliot has also believed in that it is interesting to marshal them here. Especially interesting since a parallel development of thought to many of the same ends helps to make clearer why Eliot felt the urgent necessity of fresh poetic experiment, and indicates that his reaction against the loosely prevailing standards of taste and value was not idiosyncratic but part of an emerging general state of mind.

> I prophesy that a period of dry, hard, classical verse is coming.
> The period of exhaustion seems to me to have been reached in romanticism. We shall not get any new efflorescence of verse until we get a new technique, a new convention ...
> Exactly why this dry classical spirit should have a positive and legitimate necessity to express itself in poetry is utterly inconceivable to them [i.e. to those who 'think that verse means little else than the expression of unsatisfied emotion.'] ... It [the necessity] follows from the fact that there is another quality, not the emotion produced, which is at the root of excellence in verse.
> There are then two things to distinguish, first the particular faculty of mind to see things as they really are, and apart from the conventional ways in which you have been trained to see them. This is itself rare enough in all consciousness. Second, the concentrated state of mind, the grip over oneself which is necessary in the actual expression of what one sees. To prevent one falling into the conventional curves of ingrained technique, to hold on through infinite detail and trouble to the exact curve you want. Wherever you get this sincerity, you get the fundamental quality of good art without dragging in infinite or serious.

Hulme also formulated the contrasting views of 'romanticism' and 'classicism' which Eliot has likewise followed:

> Put shortly, these are the two views, then. One, that man is intrinsically good, spoilt by circumstance; and the other that he is intrinsically limited, but disciplined by order and tradition to something fairly decent. To the one party man's nature is like a well, to the other like a bucket. The view which regards man as a well, a reservoir full of possibilities, I call the romantic; the one which regards him as a very finite and fixed creature, I call the classical.

CLEANTH BROOKS

T.S. Eliot: Thinker and Artist[1]

Eliot's career is no loose bundle of unrelated activities but possesses an essential unity. Indeed, once discovered, this unity of purpose becomes increasingly evident. Few literary men in our history have so consistently related all their activities to a coherent set of principles. And the consistency of his various writings reflects the quality of the man. In a time of disorder, Eliot moved toward a restoration of order—toward the restoration of order that poetry alone, perhaps, can give.

Thus, Eliot's fundamental reassessment of the twentieth-century literary and cultural situation was *not* expressed in his poetry alone. The poetry arose out of a mental and spiritual activity that necessarily showed itself in literary and social criticism, not only in his brilliant essays on the Elizabethan dramatists, for example, but also in a work like *Notes towards the Definition of Culture*.

When one discusses literature, few things are so deadly as the recital of abstract statements and wide generalizations. Moreover, it seems impertinent to treat a poet in this fashion, especially a poet who succeeded so brilliantly in giving his ideas concrete embodiment and who devoted so much of his discursive prose to this very split in the modern mind, this dissociation of sensibility, in which Eliot saw not only the distemper of literature but a symptom of a more general disease. Let me try to illustrate the essential unity of Eliot's work from a single topic,

From *T.S. Eliot: The Man and His Work*. First published in the *Sewanee Review* 74, no. 1 (Winter 1966). © 1966 by the University of the South. Reprinted with permission of the editor.

his treatment of the urban scene. In an essay written near the end of his life he has told us how he discovered that the urban scene was proper material for poetry, and specifically the special material for his own poetry. The passage I mean to quote begins with some observations on literary influences and what a poet can learn from earlier poets.

> Then, among influences, there are the poets from whom one has learned some one thing, perhaps of capital importance to oneself, though not necessarily the greatest contribution these poets have made. I think that from Baudelaire I learned first, a precedent for the poetical possibilities, never developed by any poet writing in my own language, the more sordid aspects of the modern metropolis, of the possibility of fusion between the sordidly realistic and the phantasmagoric, the possibility of the juxtaposition of the matter-of-fact and the fantastic. From him, as from Laforgue, I learned that the sort of material that I had, the sort of experience that an adolescent had had, in an industrial city in America, could be the material for poetry; and that the source of new poetry might be found in what had been regarded hitherto as the impossible, the sterile, the intractably unpoetic. That, in fact, the business of the poet was to make poetry out of the unexplored resources of the unpoetical; that the poet, in fact, was committed by his profession to turn the unpoetical into poetry. A great poet can give a younger poet everything that he that he has to give him in a very few lines. It may be that I am indebted to Baudelaire chiefly for half a dozen lines out of the whole of *Fleurs du Mal*; and that his significance for me is summed up in the lines:

> *Fourmillante cité, cité pleine de rêves,*
> *Où le spectre en plein jour raccroche le passant!*

I knew what *that* meant, because I had lived it before I knew that I wanted to turn it into verse on my own account.

I want to consider further both Eliot's notion that the poet, by his very profession, is committed "to turn the unpoetical into poetry", and his idea that poetry is a fusion of opposites—in this instance, a fusion of "the sordidly realistic and the phantasmagoric", of "the matter-of-fact and the fantastic".

Poetry is evidently not to be thought of as a bouquet of "poetic" objects. The implication is that the materials the poet uses are not in themselves poetic. To be agreeable or pleasant or charming is not the same thing as being poetic. Poetic value is a quality of a different order. It is not a *property* of objects but a relationship among them, a relationship discovered and established by the poet. Moreover, the relationship may be one of tension in which the materials pull against each other and resist any easy reconciliation. In this instance it is the realistic and the phantasmagoric that may seem intractable, or the matter-of-fact and the fantastic.

All of this Eliot had said before, and, because he had said it before, in this rather late essay he could afford to touch upon it lightly. But when he first enunciated this view of tension in poetry, it very much needed saying—or at least needed re-saying. And his statement of this conception, together with the poems that embodied it, inspired the literary revolution that is sometimes given Eliot's name.

It is useful to refer to another passage in which Eliot discusses the poet's use of what the Victorians sometimes regarded as hopelessly unpromising materials for poetry. The Victorian in this instance is Matthew Arnold commenting upon the ugliness of the world of Robert Burns. After quoting Arnold's rather prim observation to the effect that "no one can deny that it is of advantage to a poet to deal with a beautiful world", Eliot suddenly rounds on the nineteenth-century critic and quite flatly denies his basic assumption. The essential advantage for a poet, Eliot remarks, is *not* that of having a beautiful world with which to deal, but rather "to be able to see beneath both beauty and ugliness; to see the boredom, and the horror, and the glory". "The vision of the horror and the glory," he rather acidly concludes, "was denied to Arnold, but he knew something of the boredom."

This is excellent polemics: the hard backhand drive that rifles across the court and just dusts the opponent's back line. Yet the reader may wonder at the energy with which Eliot rejects Arnold. He may wonder too at what may seem an almost gratuitous reference to "boredom", not, surely, an obvious member of a cluster that would include "horror" and "glory". But references to boredom often come into Eliot's account of urban life, and we have in this passage mention of concerns central to his poetry.

They are indeed central to his experience of the modern metropolis where so many people find themselves caught in a world of monotonous repetition, an aimless circling without end or purpose. Eliot's early poetry is full of it:

> The morning comes to consciousness
> Of faint stale smells of beer
> From the sawdust-trampled street
> With all its muddy feet that press
> To early coffee-stands.
>
> With the other masquerades
> That time resumes,
> One thinks of all the hands
> That are raising dingy shades
> In a thousand furnished rooms.

*   *   *

> They are rattling breakfast plates in basement kitchens,
> And along the trampled edges of the street
> I am aware of the damp souls of housemaids
> Sprouting despondently at area gates.

*   *   *

> At the violet hour, the evening hour that strives
> Homeward, and brings the sailor home from sea,
> The typist home at teatime, clears her breakfast, lights
> Her stove, and lays out food in tins.
>
> Let us go, through certain half-deserted streets,
> The muttering retreats
> Of restless nights in one-night cheap hotels
> And sawdust restaurant with oyster-shells:
> Streets that follow like a tedious argument
> Of insidious intent....

The wanderer moving through the deserted city streets long past midnight walks through a genuine nightmare in which

> the floors of memory
> And all its clear relations,
> Its divisions and precisions

are dissolved, a fantastic world in which every street lamp that one passes

> Beats like a fatalistic drum ...

Yet when the wanderer turns to his own door, he steps out of one horror into a worse horror:

> The lamp said,
> 'Four o'clock,
> Here is the number on the door.
> Memory!
> You have the key,
> The little lamp spreads a ring on the stair.
> Mount.
> The bed is open; the tooth-brush hangs on the wall,
> Put your shoes at the door, sleep, prepare for life.'

> The last twist of the knife.

The wound in which this knife is twisted is modern man's loss of meaning and purpose. When life to which one expects to rise after sleep—a daylight world of clear plans and purposes—turns out to be simply a kind of automatism, as absurd as the bizarre world of the nightmare streets, the knife in the wound is given a final agonizing twist.

It may be useful to remind the reader, especially the reader who finds that Eliot's Anglo-Catholicism sticks in his craw and prevents his swallowing the poetry, that in passages of the sort that I have been quoting, we are not getting sermonizing but drama, not generalizations about facts but responses to situations, not statements about what ought to be but renditions of what is.

Eliot once remarked that prose has to do with ideals; poetry, with reality. The statement has proved puzzling to many a reader who has been brought up on just the opposite set of notions, but Eliot's observation seems to me profoundly true. Discursive prose is the medium for carrying on arguments, drawing conclusions, offering solutions. Poetry is the medium *par excellence* for rendering a total situation—for letting us know what it feels like to take a particular action or hold a particular belief or simply to look at something with imaginative sympathy.

Here are some presentations of reality—an urban vignette, a winter evening in the city:

> The winter evening settles down
> With smell of steaks in passageways.
> Six o'clock.
> The burnt-out ends of smoky days.
> And now a gusty shower wraps
> The grimy scraps
> Of withered leaves about your feet
> And newspapers from vacant lots;
> The showers beat
> On broken blinds and chimney-pots,
> And at the corner of the street
> A lonely cab-horse steams and stamps.
>
> And then the lighting of the lamps.

The Song of the third Thames-daughter:

> 'Trams and dusty trees.
> Highbury bore me. Richmond and Kew
> Undid me. By Richmond I raised my knees
> Supine on the floor of a narrow canoe.'
>
> 'My feet are at Moorgate, and my heart
> Under my feet. After the event
> He wept. He promised "a new start."
> I made no comment. What should I resent?'

'On Margate Sands.
I can connect
Nothing with nothing.
The broken fingernails of dirty hands.
My people humble people who expect
Nothing.'
                    la la

Even the raffish Sweeney's recital of his philosophy—a view of life held, incidentally, by many of Sweeney's betters—is a bit of reality too; for it is a dramatic projection of a man, not an abstract formulation. Its very rhythms testify to a personality and an attitude.

Birth, and copulation, and death.
That's all the facts when you come to brass tacks:
Birth, and copulation, and death.
I've been born, and once is enough.

Readers have responded powerfully to such passages, even readers who hold very different conceptions of what the world ought to be. What is primarily at stake in all these passages is not the reader's approval or rejection of a statement, but his response to authentic reality. The only compulsion to respond is that exerted by the authority of the imagination. Perhaps the poet can never do more than exert such authority; but in any case he cannot afford to do less.

This matter of the reader's response has another and more special aspect. Eliot suggests that many of those who live in the modern world have been drugged and numbed by it. One task of the poet is to penetrate their torpor, to awaken them to full consciousness of their condition, to let them see where they are. The theme recurs throughout Eliot's poetry from the earliest poems to the latest.

The people who inhabit *The Waste Land* cling to their partial oblivion. They say:

Winter kept us warm, covering
Earth in forgetful snow, feeding
A little life with dried tubers.

Or like the old women of Canterbury, they may say:

> We do not wish anything to happen.
> Seven years we have lived quietly,
> Succeeded in avoiding notice,
> Living and partly living.

The trivial daily actions, they point out, at least marked

> a limit to our suffering.
> Every horror had its definition,
> Every sorrow had a kind of end....

What they dread now is the "disturbance" of the seasons, the decisive break in the numbing routine that will wake them out of their half-life.

But the partially numbed creatures may be, and usually are, people of the contemporary world. They may, for example, be like the characters in *The Family Reunion* who do not want anything to rumple their rather carefully arranged lives—who want things to be "normal"—and who cannot see that—to use their nephew's words—the event that they call normal "is merely the unreal and the unimportant".

They may be like certain well-bred inhabitants of Boston, Massachusetts:

> ... evening quickens faintly in the street
> Wakening the appetite of life in some
> And to others bringing the *Boston Evening Transcript*....

Or they may be the bored drawing-room characters in "The Love Song of J. Alfred Prufrock" whom Prufrock would like to confront with the truth about themselves. He would like to say to them:

> 'I am Lazarus, come from the dead,
> Come back to tell you all, I shall tell you all'....

But he well knows that these overcivilized and desiccated people would not be impressed by the Lazarus of the New Testament, much less by a self-conscious man "with a bald spot in the middle of [his] hair", a man aware of the fact that he wears a "necktie rich and modest, but asserted by a simple pin". In any case, these people would not understand the talk of a man who had experienced real death or real life.

The themes that run through so much of Eliot's poetry—life that is only a half-life because it cannot come to terms with death, the liberation into true living that comes from the acceptance of death, the ecstatic moment that partakes of both life and death:

> ... I could not
> Speak, and my eyes failed, I was neither
> Living nor dead, and I knew nothing,
> Looking into the heart of light, the silence.

These and the other themes that recur in Eliot's poetry bear the closest relation to his concern with the boredom and the horror and the glory that he finds in our contemporary metropolitan life. They also bear the closest relationship to the sense of unreality that pervades a world that has lost the rhythm of the seasons, has lost any sense of community, and, most of all, has lost a sense of purpose. Such a world is unreal: the sordid and the matter-of-fact do not erase the phantasmagoric but accentuate it. The spectre does indeed in broad daylight reach out to grasp the passer-by. London, "under the brown fog of a winter noon" as well as "under the brown fog of a winter dawn", is seen as an "Unreal City", and the crowds flowing across London Bridge might be in Dante's Hell:

> I had not thought death had undone so many.
> Sighs, short and infrequent, were exhaled,
> And each man fixed his eyes before his feet.

The echo of *The Divine Comedy* is not merely a flourish or an attempt to touch up the modern scene by giving it literary overtones. What connects the modern scene with Dante's "Inferno" is the poet's insight into the nature of hell. The man who sees the crowds flowing over London Bridge as damned souls, if challenged for putting them thus into hell, might justify his observation by paraphrasing a line from Christopher Marlowe: "Why, this is hell, nor are they out of it."

In view of the complaint that Eliot sighs after vanished glories, sentimentalizes the past, and hates the present, one must insist on Eliot's

ability to dramatize the urban reality with honesty and sensitivity. If the
world about which we must write has lost the rhythm of the seasons,
then the poet must be open to the new rhythms so that he can relate
them to the old. Eliot once wrote that the poet must be able to use the
rhythms of the gasoline engine:

> At the violet hour, when the eyes and back
> Turn upward from the desk, when the human engine waits,
> Like a taxi throbbing waiting....

If the modern world has lost its sense of community, the poet must
present that loss not as a generalization but as a dramatic rendition, not
as observed from the outside but as felt from the inside. He has done so
not only in the nightmare passages of *The Waste Land*—

> There is not even solitude in the mountains
> But red sullen faces sneer and snarl
> From doors of mudcracked houses—

but also in the realistic passages:

> 'My nerves are bad to-night. Yes, bad. Stay with me.
> 'Speak to me. Why do you never speak. Speak.
>   'What are you thinking of? What thinking? What?
> 'I never know what you are thinking. Think.'

But he has also on occasion rendered the sense of community in positive
terms—not as something lost but as a present reality:

> O City city, I can sometimes hear
> Beside a public bar in Lower Thames Street,
> The pleasant whining of a mandoline
> And a clatter and a chatter from within
> Where fishmen lounge at noon....

As for the sense of loss of purpose, that loss is never merely asserted but
always rendered concretely. It occurs so frequently in Eliot's poetry that
it hardly needs illustration. Indeed, it may be best in this instance to take

the illustration from Joseph Conrad's *Heart of Darkness*, a story that lies behind so much of Eliot's early poetry. Marlow, the character who relates the story, finds many of his experiences tinged with unreality. As he makes his way to the African coast and then on up the Congo to try to locate Kurtz, his sense of unreality is magnified—not merely because the jungle seems fantastic, but because the civilized characters he meets are disoriented, obsessed, and thus absurd. One object stands out sharply from this miasma of unreality. Marlow finds in an abandoned hut "an old tattered book, entitled *An Inquiry into Some Points of Seamanship*, by a man Tower, Towson—some such name.... Not a very enthralling book; but at the first glance you could see there a singleness of intention ... which made these humble pages ... luminous with another than a professional light.... [The book] made me forget the jungle and the [ivory-seeking] pilgrims in a delicious sensation of having come upon something unmistakeably real." It seems so because it is instinct with purpose—because, to use Marlow's words, you could see in it "an honest concern for the right way of going to work". This is why the book shines with the light of reality.

The sense of unreality is also associated with the vision of a world that is disintegrating. In *The Waste Land*, the cities of a disintegrating civilization seem unreal as if they were part of a mirage. The parched traveler asks:

> What is the city over the mountains
> Cracks and reforms and bursts in the violet air
> Falling towers—

but these cities are also like a mirage in that they are inverted, are seen as upside-down; and the passage that follows shows everything turned topsy-turvy:

> ... bats with baby faces in the violet light
> Whistled, and beat their wings
> And crawled head downward down a blackened wall
> And upside down in air were towers
> Tolling reminiscent bells, that kept the hours
> And voices singing out of empty cisterns and exhausted wells.

Eliot also uses the empty whirl in order to suggest the break-up of civilization. Toward the end of "Gerontion" we have such a vision, people whose surnames suggest that the disintegration is international and worldwide: De Bailhache, Fresca, and Mrs. Cammel are whirled

> Beyond the circuit of the shuddering Bear
> In fractured atoms.

Though "Gerontion" was written long before the explosion of the first atomic bomb, I suppose there is some temptation nowadays to read into the passage our present unease and to regard the fractured atoms into which humankind has been vaporized as the debris of an atomic war. But I doubt that Mr. Eliot ever changed his opinion about the way the world ends.

"The Hollow Men", who know in their hollow hearts that they are not really "lost / Violent souls", but only "stuffed men", sing

> *This is the way the world ends*
> *This is the way the world ends*
> *This is the way the world ends*
> *Not with a bang but a whimper.*

The vortex in which De Bailhache, Fresca, and Mrs. Cammel are caught is essentially described in "Burnt Norton":

> Men and bits of paper, whirled by the cold wind
> That blows before and after time....

With the empty whirl, the purposeless moving in a circle, we are back once more to the theme of boredom, and there is a good deal of evidence that Eliot did indeed see in such torpor and apathy the real dying out of a civilization. In 1934, for example, he wrote: "Without religion the whole human race would die, as according to W. H. R. Rivers, some Melanesian tribes have died, solely of boredom." This is a polemical passage out of a polemical essay, but we need not discount the idea merely for that reason. It is an integral part of Eliot's thinking. It is to be found everywhere in his prose and poetry—even in a poem like *Sweeney Agonistes*, where we have the following spoof on the cinematic stereotype of the golden age, life on a South Sea island:

Where the Gauguin maids
In the banyan shades
Wear palmleaf drapery
Under the bam
Under the boo
Under the bamboo tree.

Tell me in what part of the wood
Do you want to flirt with me?
Under the breadfruit, banyan, palmleaf
Or under the bamboo tree?
Any old tree will do for me
Any old wood is just as good
Any old isle is just my style
Any fresh egg
Any fresh egg
And the sound of the coral sea.

Doris protests that she doesn't like eggs and doesn't like life on "your crocodile isle". And when the singers renew their account of the delights of such a life, Doris replies:

That's not life, that's no life
Why I'd just as soon be dead.

Doris is a young woman who is clearly no better than she should be, but in this essential matter, she shows a great deal more discernment than J. Alfred Prufrock's companions, the ladies who "come and go / Talking of Michelangelo".

I have tried to suggest how the themes and images of Eliot's poetry are related to his convictions about the nature of our present-day civilization. But I shall have badly confused matters if in doing so I have seemed to reduce his poetry to a kind of thin and brittle propaganda for a particular world view. The primary role of poetry is to give us an account of reality, not to argue means for reshaping it. To be more specific: if a culture is sick, the poet's primary task is to provide us with a diagnosis, not to prescribe a specific remedy. For all of his intense interest in the problems of our culture, and in spite of the fact that he himself was deeply committed to a doctrinal religion, Eliot was careful never to confuse poetry with politics or with religion. The loss of a sense of purpose, the conviction that one is simply going round in a circle, is an experience that many of the readers of Eliot's poetry have recognized as their own; but in their decisions as to what to do about it, such readers have differed as much as the Christian differs from the atheistic existentialist. To get out of the circle, to find one's proper end and begin to walk toward it—this is a matter of the highest importance, work for the statesman, the sage, and the saint; but Eliot was too modest ever to claim any of these roles for himself, and he was as well aware as anyone of the confusion of tongues that makes it difficult for men of our century to agree on what the proper goal is. At any rate, he argued the case for what he took to be the true goal, not in his poetry, but in his prose.

In a time of grave disorder, Eliot has moved toward a restoration of order. Not the least important part of this work of restoration has been to clarify the role of poetry, not claiming so much for it that it is transformed into prophecy, or Promethean politics, or an ersatz religion; but at the same time pointing out its unique and irreplaceable function and defending its proper autonomy.

Genuine poetry, seen in its proper role, performing for us what only it can perform, does contribute to the health of a culture. A first step toward the recovery of the health of our culture may well be the writing of a poetry that tells us the truth about ourselves in our present situation, that is capable of dealing with the present world, that does not have to leave out the boredom and the horror of our world in order to discern its true glory. More modestly still, a poetry that can deal with the clutter of language in an age of advertising and propaganda restores to that degree the health of language.

Eliot was well aware of this problem. Advertising and propaganda were for him instruments for "influencing ... masses of men" by means other than "their intelligence". And he once went so far as to say: "You have only to examine the mass of newspaper leading articles, the mass of political exhortation, to appreciate the fact that good prose cannot be written by a people without convictions."

The difficulty of writing good prose in our era extends to other kinds of writing, including poetry. Of this too, Eliot was aware. In *The Rock*, he has the chorus assert that "The soul of Man must quicken to creation"—not only to create new forms, colors, and music but so that

Out of the slimy mud of words, out of the sleet and hail of
    verbal imprecisions,
Approximate thoughts and feelings, words that have taken
    the place of thoughts and feelings,
... [may] spring the perfect order of speech, and the beauty
    of incantation.

In a later and finer poem, he puts this ideal of style more precisely and more memorably still, and he makes this ideal structure of the language a model of that thing which men must try to accomplish in their lives. It is Eliot's description of the relation that obtains among the words that make up a passage luminous with meaning. In it,

    ... every word is at home,
Taking its place to support the others,
The word neither diffident nor ostentatious,
An easy commerce of the old and the new,
The common word exact without vulgarity,
The formal word precise but not pedantic,
The complete consort dancing together....

These beautiful lines celebrate the poet's victory over disorder, the peculiar triumph possible to a master of language. They describe what Eliot actually achieved many times in his own poetry. They provide an emblem of the kind of harmony that ought to obtain in wider realms—in the just society and in the true community.

NOTE

1. A lecture given at Eliot College, University of Kent at Canterbury, December 10, 1965.

CHARLES ALTIERI

Eliot's Impact on Twentieth-Century Anglo-American Poetry

When I was asked to write on the figure of Eliot in modern poetry I thought of several reasons not to accept. On a personal level I could imagine no way that such critical work would not reveal more about my limitations than about Eliot's powers, since I would miss or mistake crucial aspects of his heritage. And on a theoretical level I deeply mistrust any study claiming to speak of influences. Where such studies are not obvious, they tend to rely on loose speculations about specific echoes or to invoke problematic analogies attempting to establish one writer's shaping overall projects for another.

Yet here I am. The theoretical problem quickly became a challenge to test a concept of impact that might avoid the problems worrying me, since impact is less a matter of one poet deliberately engaging another than it is a matter of the currency of ideas and of a logic informing how writers shape ambitions or develop styles. Thus we shift from trying to inhabit the mind of specific writers to attempting to describe a theater in which Eliot becomes a stimulus focussing a range of possible investments in versions of his work. And then we also shift the personal stakes. My fears did not subside, but they were outweighed by the opportunity to take responsibility for my own love of Eliot: I could ask how and why the now dominant account misses much that was, and is, culturally vital in Eliot's work; and I could use the reception of Eliot's

From *The Cambridge Companion to T.S. Eliot*, ed. A. David Moody. © 1994 by Cambridge University Press. Reprinted by permission.

113

work by other poets to make clear what in his work does not yield to appropriation or modification, but marks instead his still distinctive modernist voice.[1]

I

From a historical perspective we must say that there have been many T. S. Eliots, linked at best by family resemblance. But for our purposes we must be content with two basic characters bearing that name, each the hero of a quite different story. The first story dominated for four decades. It cast Eliot as the American poet who brought Anglo-American poetry into the modern age by forcing it to encounter urban life, by refusing sentimental idealizations in pursuit of the mind's intricate evasions and slippages, and by intensely engaging the various modes of victimage fundamental to contemporary culture. But this story never quite escaped its demonic other—now told both by those who think Eliot's modernism was an élitist destruction of still viable poetic traditions and by those like the LANGUAGE Poets appalled by his conservatism in every domain. Here Eliot becomes a colonizing modernist forcing on poetry the anxieties and powerless learning of a dying white European culture and imposing a style that could provide no alternative to the paralysis it recorded.

Let me start with this second story, then try to define its limitations. Its first strong statement occurs in William Carlos Williams's 1920 "Prologue" to *Kora In Hell*: "Upon the Jepson filet Eliot balances his mushroom ... If to do this, if to be a Whistler at best, in the art of poetry, is to reach the height of poetic expression then Ezra and Eliot have approached it and *tant pis* for the rest of us." But it took *The Waste Land* and thirty more years of brooding to foster Williams's retrospective statement that most fully established the case against Eliot as the prematurely established Goliath against which young Davids must prove themselves:

> I felt at once that it had set me back twenty years, and I'm sure it did. Critically Eliot returned us to the classroom just at the moment when I felt that we were on the point of an escape to matters much closer to the essence of a new art form itself—rooted in the locality which should give it fruit. I knew at once that in certain ways I was most defeated.[2]

For Williams, Eliot's major weakness was his relying on an abstract sense of culture, ungrounded in any actual communities or practices so that it became a constant source of snobbism on the one hand, anxiety and paralysis on the other. Without a sense of the local there could be no objects for consciousness which could directly engage the full energies of one's medium; there could only be the infinite regresses of the mind seeking to find within its own activity some rest or cure of the ground.

Such sentiments may have cost Williams dearly, since he spent much of his later career working against the grain of his own talent in the hope that he could rival Eliot's status as culture hero and poet-theorist. But he also saw clearly the basic outlines that future versions of this story would take—from Yeats on Eliot's merely "satiric intensity," to Auden's desire to replace a poetics of image and gyre by one devoted to principles of care and of community, to Karl Shapiro's critique of Eliot's élitist bookishness, to the strange conjunction leading two rival anthologies in the early 1960s, each to justify itself by opposition to Eliot on impersonality and his effects on the New Criticism. Then in recent criticism we find much the same lines redrawn in somewhat different languages—for example in Hugh Kenner's claims for Pound over Eliot on the grounds that where Eliot has only the symbolist mind in endless pursuit of itself Pound binds poetry to the facts of nature and history, in Marjorie Perloff's contrast between a poetics of symbolist lyric closure and a pursuit of Rimbaud's indeterminate and overflowing transformative energies, and in almost everyone's worries about Eliot's conservatism in politics and in religion.[3] And finally there is emerging a sociological version of these same principles that emphasizes the ways in which Eliot's modernism served larger establishment interests. As Orwell shrewdly observed, Eliot could make a radical modernism in the arts feasible for arbiters of cultural taste and for literary education because he connected it not only to the very tradition it challenged but also to an adamantly conservative politics.[4] Eliot's experimental traditionalism managed to expose the tenuous cultural role of the cultural establishment in the very process of offering it new tokens of its hegemony.

But even if one accepts all these criticisms, as I do, I think one must also ask if such a summary can come even close to understanding what Eliot actually meant to twentieth-century poetry. These critical attitudes grasp what is limited in Eliot, but not what seemed to become possible through him. For that we must turn back to the first story—to grasp its elements, to understand why these elements lost their force in modern culture, and perhaps to see beyond the now dominant versions of those elements. Let us then balance Williams's reaction to Eliot with Hart Crane's. As irritated as Williams by Eliot's pretensions as well as by his pervasive despondency, Crane none the less realized as early as 1919 that for even an alternative poetry to be fully modern it would have to go "through" Eliot "toward a different goal":

> You see it is just such a fearful temptation to imitate him that at times I have been almost distracted ... In his own realm Eliot presents us with an absolute impasse, yet oddly enough he can be utilized to lead us to, intelligently point to, other positions and "pastures new."

Then another letter puts the case more specifically, "I would apply as much of his erudition and technique as I can absorb and assemble toward a more positive, or ... ecstatic goal."[5]

One could find similar statements in poets like Auden, Tate, Jones, and Lowell. Part of their excitement was technical. Eliot simply provided new ways of assuming voices, registering details, adapting speech rhythms and putting elements together within poems. But his greatest genius, and greatest impact, lay in the ways that he allowed poets to cast technical experiment as significant cultural work struggling to make poetry a dynamic force for cultural change. As Louise Bogan put it, Eliot "swung the balance over from whimpering German bucolics to forms within which contemporary complexity could find expression."[6] And as almost all early commentators on Eliot remarked, this sense of cultural work took two basic forms: Eliot showed that poetry could enter the city, enter those sites most obviously subject to everything destructive in modernity, and thus could provide intimate access to the costs of consciousness at odds with itself as it tried to engage what modernity seemed to demand. But even more important was the complex relation between the states of victim and visionary that in Eliot's poetry seemed inseparable from one another. Forced to take responsibility for his own historicity, Eliot could not escape the danger of exposing how deeply he, and perhaps the poetic imagination itself, had become complicit in what they proposed to cure. But the greater the sense of victimage, the more intense the haunting prospect that there would emerge an imaginative site where we could at least glimpse an "infinitely gentle, infinitely suffering thing," able to resist our ironies.

To study Eliot's impact is to analyze the appeal and the threats presented by the basic sites which this feeling of being a victim enabled him to construct. As an initial mapping I want to concentrate on the force and the fate of Eliot's two most influential critical concepts—his claims about the dissociation of sensibility that had dominated European thought since the seventeenth century and his insistence on an impersonality that could combat that dissociation by treating art works as objective correlatives rather than as personal expressions or rhetorical performances. This should help clarify the appeal of both stories about him, and it should allow us finally to turn to how the poetry itself both extends the force of those enabling concepts, and retains capacities to affect poets even after the ideas have become antiquarian curiosities.

It seems impossible now to recover the immense appeal of the first of these concepts, perhaps because for us only questions about individuals, not about cultures, seem to have any urgency, or any consequences for action. But for Eliot's age his critical claims about the dissociation of sensibility set the stage for everything else, primarily by foregrounding the interplay between suffering and vision dramatized in his poetry. First it made victimage heroic by posing the modernist poet as one who lives fully the deep contradictions plaguing the West since the seventeenth century. Even more important, it dignified the poet's positive roles by affording a principle for cultural analysis that based a culture's health on the states of spirit or psychic economies that it could sustain. Facing Hart Crane's breakdown, Tate would think not of economic matters, not even of psychoanalytic, biographical contexts, but of the general cultural collapse of any possible harmony between thinking and feeling: Crane's career becomes a "vindication of Eliot's major premise—that the integrity of the individual consciousness has broken down."[7] And then, once the health of the psyche is understood as a spiritual reflection of cultural conditions, poetry takes on enormous significance as a possible means of at once registering disease and testing the possibility for cure. Therefore while Eliot could find a vantage for criticizing Romanticism as little more than puritanism basing its inwardness on nature, he could also appeal to the fundamental emotional consolation Romanticism offered: only by narcissistic self-absorption could one turn one's own anxieties into representative cultural symptoms that one could then hope to combat by imaginative means.

This relation to Romanticism gave Eliot a position for writers much like that which theorists of abstraction occupied for modernist painting. By criticizing the very ideal of representation the painters set themselves up as combatting not simply previous styles but a general cultural plight created by the willful egotism of Renaissance ideals, with their corresponding denial of the demonic and daemonic forces which resist representation. Eliot gave poets a comparable sense of their own world-historical task by inviting them to combat what seemed the very formation of Europe's psyche. Each poet's sufferings were not simply personal; they were representative—impotence conferred power. And each poet's efforts to express the complexity of contemporary life became a possible remaking of what we could take ourselves to be and of what futures we could imagine for the race. Writing need no longer be a matter of personal expression or the exchanges of refilled sensibilities or the exploration of the powers of aesthetic contemplation. The imagination was neither a mode of escape nor an instrument for aesthetic pleasure. Through it writers had the power to invent and test aspects of psychic economies charged with the need to find means of facing up to the terrors of modernity, and propelled by the dream that some ways of facing up might actually open new paths for a culture stuck in destructive habits. Thus Eliot's foregrounding of the dissociation of sensibility did for poetry what Marx's concept of alienation did for historical analysis: the terms of suffering became the keys to understanding how deep change might be possible.

But how does one combat this dissociation? One must begin by grappling with its most destructive manifestations—which for Eliot consisted in substituting a faith in personal feelings for what Bradley had taught him were the more comprehensive frameworks that enclosed the person within complex social and intellectual webs. Therefore Eliot tried to idealize principles of impersonality that would force people to see themselves from the outside, and hence to recognize both the limits of their imaginary projections about themselves and the structural forces binding them to those projections. And, more important, impersonality might help free art from our ideas of sensibility, since rather than assume we could identify with speakers, we would confront "impressions and experiences combine[d] in peculiar and unexpected ways."[8] Perhaps by an "escape from personality" we might find different ways to experience both our dependencies and our powers as historical agents. Thus Eliot applied to modern cultural wars the formalist impulse developed by Kant and given lyrical force within symbolism: instead of connecting art directly to the expressive desires of its maker, the work is asked to serve as a distinctive mode of thinking. The formal syntax does a good deal of the motivating that moves the text from detail to detail, and it, not some expressive will, has the power to elicit complexes of feeling which may allow some freedom from those narrative structures contaminated by the dissociation of sensibility. Consequently one can claim for the poem both an extraordinary subtlety and an extraordinary comprehensiveness, since the principles of closure can be as capacious and discriminating as in any other mode of impersonal, and hence transpersonal, thinking.

Now a second difficult question emerges. How can these projections beyond the personality take on cultural force? As we try to respond, we find ourselves having to confront serious problems both within Eliot and within those who tried to mediate his work, so that our story about stories about Eliot comes full circle and we see why the negative version managed to prevail. Eliot's own early poetry could only manage impersonality as an aspect of the dissociation of sensibility, so that rather than providing a cure it became the deepest symptom of the disease. For when the mind seeks such distance from the energies that put it into motion, it finds it almost impossible to escape what I call the "pathos of reflective distance" characterizing his first two volumes. There the intensity and clarity of Eliot's lines oddly isolate the speaking from the speaker, perhaps from any possibility of correlating an agent's investments in a particular life and particular body with the structure for reflection that persons must employ—hence the "shadow" in *The Hollow Men*. Eliot seems fascinated by those moments in which the mind is paralyzed by its own lucid grasp of itself, so that it simultaneously has the last word and realizes that it has no word that can mediate the person's own specific investments in the very processes being enacted. Notice, for example, how chilling, how disembodied, the incredible precision of these lines from "Gerontion" that seem to insist on the gulf between the imperative to think and the possibilities of investing in the mind's actions:

After such knowledge, what forgiveness?
Think now History has many cunning passages, contrived
    corridors ...
She gives when our attention is distracted
And what she gives, gives with such supple confusions
that the giving famishes the craving ...
                                                    Think
Neither fear nor courage saves us. Unnatural vices
Are fathered by our heroism. Virtues
are forced upon us by our impudent crimes.

With Eliot's work so slippery, and so ready to undo his positive
projections, a serious burden falls on those heirs most drawn to his
enterprise. Like Crane they felt they had to use impersonality against
dissociation without succumbing to an idealization of irony that only
repeats the dissociation in more virulent form. And many of them
wanted to develop a full theoretical and pedagogical account translating
Eliot's idiosyncratically intricate and subtle mind into principles that
could put his blend of wishes and insights on what seemed a firm
foundation. In both cases Eliot's power of concrete imagination gave way
to Eliot the culture figure, and there began both the kind of
representation and the need for reaction which made him ultimately a
widespread object of resentment. The work of the New Critics makes
the process obvious. In systematizing Eliot they also oversimplified
him—consolidating his power but also ultimately offering a sacrificial
victim for those who recognized the need to overthrow this version of
that power. Where Eliot treated the poetic site as a literal construction
of possible modes of agency, these critics emphasized the textual,
semantic properties of the site. That then led to casting the force of
agency within the poem almost entirely in semantic terms that occluded
the cultural roles Eliot hoped his impersonality might open up.
Impersonal authorship (later to become *textualité*) allowed a multiplying
of meanings through a focus on paradox and elaborate conceit. But then
to explain how these meanings might be integrated, New Critical theory
had to rely on tracing formal relationships and locating their resonance
in terms of tragic ironies which only art could provide as the mark of its
distance from the life where differences constantly slip into inescapable
rigid oppositions. Even the excruciating tensions generated by the

pathos of distance became fundamentally semantic properties so that the dynamic divisions between voice and intelligence become less important than the capacity of an ironic authorial presence to contain the whole within certain patterns and mythic echoes. So what seemed capable of transforming life became confined to aesthetic attitudes. The passionate becomes the bookish; and criteria of intensity and intricacy give way to concerns for comprehensiveness and tragic composure.

II

To get back behind New Criticism, and to recapture the specific impact of Eliot's passions on generations of poets, we must now shift from the domain of ideas to that of concrete lyric effects. Once again we must deal with several Eliots—minimally the very different figures who fused symbolist abstraction with the desiccated impressionism of poems like "Preludes," who explored mythic landscape in *The Waste Land*, and who struggled in *Four Quartets* to bring a new personal directness and intensity to the modernist lyric. And we must cover a great deal of material in a small amount of space, so I will have to be quite elliptical, trusting to the reader's familiarity with Eliot and his critics for the evidence that my generalizations are well founded.

For Eliot's initial impact we must place ourselves within the world of late Victorian and Georgian poetry, as if for the first time confronting the opening of "Prufrock":

> Let us go then, you and I,
> When the evening is spread out against the sky
> Like a patient etherized upon a table;
> Let us go, through certain half-deserted streets,
> The muttering retreats
> Of restless nights in one-night cheap hotels ...

It is the wary indirectness that seems most striking, as if for the first time poetry took account of a cultural situation in which the straightforward interpretation of situations and the direct assertion of emotions had come to seem hollow, impotent, and self-deluding. The very effort to address one's audience and define social relations objectively seemed instead to require registering the displacing force of one's own unmastered desires. And then subjective personality takes on a new, and terrifying force. To come to self-consciousness is to find oneself irreducibly in dialogue with one's projections of an other, equally part of one's subjective life, and equally destabilized. The poem's speaker does attempt to harmonize those psychic roles by turning to description, hoping that the gesture outward might provide common ground. Yet even the effort at description is so warped by the speaker's divided psyche that the attempt at communication only intensifies the pressure from within. Prufrock needs metaphors to express that scene, only to find the metaphors imposing, their own violent displacements. This process of displacement begins casually, with the vague figure of evening "spread out against the sky." But the vagueness is enough to open the gates for Prufrock's disturbed sensibility: "spread out" generates a bizarre pathetic fallacy in which the evening takes on the agency of all etherized patient. Then the descriptive focus returns, only to have the half-deserted streets modulate back into both literal and figurative retreats evoked by Prufrock's loneliness.

In this world there is no possibility of adequate description of self-possession through one's art. Fact turns into image, and image forces upon the scene all the pains of the agent's experience of subjectivity. This, we might say, is lyric poetry's rendering of the realities of dissociated sensibility, realities that require turning the poet's skills to the undoing of any dream of thinking as mastery. Instead the poet's self-consciousness is inseparable from the poet's pathos. The fusing of city and psyche traps the artist in an "inner world of nightmare" that demands an aura of intimacy and vulnerability leading ultimately to confessional styles as foreign in principle to Eliot, as they are close to some of his work in affective range. Who is Berryman's Henry but Prufrock with American edges? And Lowell and Plath make powerful use of Eliot's model by which the extremities of voice become a guarantee of access to the deepest registers of the psyche.

So we find in poetry a new pathos, based less on self-exposure than on an excruciatingly fine intelligence at odds with itself. And we find that promise of a new intimacy inseparable from the challenge to take on the mind's intricate dialogues with itself. This intimacy in turn offered three significant sets of resources for those reading Eliot carefully, resources which his subsequent work would both extend and modify. First, this work opens Anglo-American poetry to a strange conjunction between an extraordinarily precise diction (almost parodic in the quatrain poems, but deeply telling in "Gerontion" and later work) and a wide range of expressive effects, much as contemporaneous German painting used its suspicions about realistic representation to broaden the psychological materials that could be given painterly renderings. For Williams, self-consciousness about syntax became the bearer of modernist foregrounding of the medium. That innovation, however, could be seen as limiting poetry to modes of perception and immediate valuation. But Eliot's precision of diction opened several directions—from introducing new complexities to persona poems, where diction is character, to sustaining the kind of discursive lyricism explored by Auden and Tate. More important, poets could make that extravagant attention to diction also a license for an extravagance of vision. Thus we find Auden, according to Edward Mendelson, discovering that since a modern poetry could be "comic and grotesque," "the extravagance of his personality was for the first time free to disport in his verse."[9]

Eliot's second major innovation extends this tension between precisions and extravagance into complex authorial states. Imagine precision as an objectifying strategy, extravagance as the irreducible pressure of subjective fantasy. Then notice what happens when each pole goes to an extreme: the objective takes on an excess that comes to appear an inescapable residue of subjective intensities, and the subjective seems driven by forces from beyond the self that it cannot control. In Eliot's characteristic lyric states these poles of subject and of object continually slide into one another, so that it seems impossible to make any firm distinctions between scene and act, or figuratively, between foreground and background. Poetically the impact of this is as obvious and as widespread as it is important: all descriptive impulses had to pass through the intricate evasions of the psyche. For now though the quickest way to appreciate what is involved is to turn to Eliot's basic concept for these effects—the concept of objective correlative.

Like the other major modernists, Eliot saw that if there cannot be clear objectivity about the world, art must turn constructivist. It must promise not truth but completeness by trying to make visible those psychological energies which constantly displace what both descriptive and mimetic versions of the dramatic attempt to stabilize; and it must hope that such an art can so define authorial agency that its contingency within history will seem less of a burden, more a principle of testimony.

Poetry then had to be impersonal and complex—not because such attributes secured the authority of culture but because the poet needed means of resisting the illusory authority of both the poet's descriptive capacities and his or her seductive personality. For Eliot the ideal of an objective correlative offered a way of showing how a constructivist aesthetic could none the less bear a profoundly self-divided and even self-cancelling poetic imagination. By conceiving of the poem as an objective correlative for emotions, rather than a direct expression of them, Eliot could envision writing as an effort to render psychic forces in conflict, without having to succumb to any single version of a speaking presence working, as Prufrock does, to secure imaginary versions of the self which in fact miss half of what is happening in the very process of seeking closure.

The result is what we might call a new immediacy, a new literalness, and a new abstract intimacy for poetry, all of which require resisting traditional ideas of self so that the concrete textures of poetry can provide richer imaginative alternatives. Similarly, the New Critics' ideals of organic unity prove a poor substitute for the density of internal relationships Eliot's poetry establishes, since those ideals make semantic categories more important than the density and complexity Eliot focused on. But the best poets saw better than the critics, as we can observe in the way poems like Crane's "At Melville's Tomb," begin from a point of view so deeply internalized that entering it requires a leap of imaginative faith:

> Often beneath the wave, wide from this ledge
> The dice of drowned men's bones he saw bequeath
> An embassy.

Even more eloquent testimony to the difference Eliot makes in this regard comes from a novelist, Virginia Woolf:

> The [new modern] poets express a feeling that is actually being made and torn out of us at the moment. One does not recognize it in the first place; often for some reason one fears it; one watches it with keenness and compares it jealously and suspiciously with the old feeling that one knew. Hence the difficulty of modern poetry; and it is because of this difficulty

that one cannot remember more than two consecutive lines of any good modern poet.[10]

The objective correlative is inseparable from Eliot's ideal of impersonality. But by coming to impersonality along this route I think we can appreciate how Eliot's version of it constitutes the third major factor in his impact on other poets. Impersonality is not primarily a defensive strategy or élitist displacement of the social by abstract cultural contexts. Rather it provides a means for elaborating and intensifying the fluid intimacy that Eliot achieves by imagining poems as literal sites where complexes of feeling play against fantasies of selfhood. This is most evident in *The Waste Land*, where we might say Eliot tried to make the impersonal play the dramatic role usually granted to specific speakers. Here the entire effort is to get beyond single lyric personality to a mode of reflection treating the scenic level of the poem as the direct rendering of collective experience. One might say that the ideal of impersonal complexes of feeling, or, better, of the effort to win impersonality from the ego's efforts to impose itself as the arbiter for the energies of personality, provides the necessary link blending the various modes of Eliot's earlier work into the state somewhere between obsession and prayer that characterizes the mythic mindscape of *The Waste Land*. In the earlier writing we find Prufrock's psychological pathos conjoined with poems like "Preludes" that tease out the unbearable tensions between what can and cannot be objectified; then we see those states abstracted into the surreal spaces of the quatrain poems. *The Waste Land* does not quite integrate these modes, but it does put them into conjunctions that reveal the unsatisfied desires underlying them and the possibility, almost entirely destroyed, of a spiritual life available in the interstices of all our expressive vehicles. Literalness to the emotional complexes beneath our ideas of selves opens for poetry the possibility of a romance of the negative, of the interstitial, important to poets like John Ashbery, Ann Lauterbach, Louise Gluck, and Jorie Graham.

Such literalness can take on substantial metaphysical and political implications, now free of the forms of coherence imposed by what Charles Olson would call "the interference of the lyrical ego." On the simplest level impersonality is inseparable from those experiments in juxtaposition that allied Eliot with the collage principles being elaborated in the visual arts.[11] Juxtaposition announces a break with traditional modes of correlating information, both on the level of public argument and, more important, on the level of personal psychological investments. Then it forces us to ask what modes of coherence can take their place. This is not a question that can be answered directly, without turning juxtaposition into simply a vehicle for other forms of argument. Instead the question works as a pressure which makes us attend to the edges of what is conjoined, as if there one could enter modes of relationship deeper than any descriptive language could provide. If we look backward from John Ashbery, the contemporary poet who I think is most responsive to Eliot's example, we can postulate for Eliot something like a semantic transformation of symbolist ideals of the music of poetry: we are invited to listen for what crosses the gaps in the poems and sets up rhythms of feeling, so that the ontology of music takes on a kind of semantic force, seeming to approximate the mind's own deep structure of needs.

In Eliot's poetry this music sustains a dramatic play in which ghostly echoes both open and bridge the constant unmaking of sense into pregnant gaps which we cannot but attempt to fill, even as we know that our efforts can do nothing more than reveal partial understandings opening ourselves to experiencing meaning as a mode of grace. Perhaps only the Joyce of *Finnegans Wake* fully understood the moral and psychological implications of Eliot's mythic method. But all the most ambitious modernists, from Crane, to David Jones, to Seamus Heaney, to Merrill's pastiche version of Eliotic musical necromancy, would take up the basic quest to have ghosts fill the necessary gaps in our experience of meaning. And an even larger contingent would learn from Eliot how the allusions elicited by these ghostly presences highlighted the historicity of their own poetic activity. Allusions necessarily position the author within a set of historical factors: they afford a means of denying the traditional atemporality of lyric states while also invoking that condition as an aura of possible depths underlying the historical differences that the allusions indicate. And allusion foregrounds the poet's accepting the historical task of constructing ideal readers, or at least of reminding real readers of a dimension for idealization within their actual practices. Allusions create the sense that there is a common cultural perspective from which the different levels of historical existence within the poem can be understood and assessed, while also challenging poets to push their readers beyond conditions of immediate response so that they will reflect on their own positioning within history, and hence compose a site beyond the immediate event.

Finally I must just touch upon a feature of Eliot's exploration of impersonality which would take us in an entirely different direction. Ultimately Eliot rejected both impersonality and its attendant culturalism because he saw that by seeking comprehensiveness one only insured a constant emptiness, frustrated by endlessly receding spiritual possibilities. There could be no adequate ground discovered in seeking cultural universals, and there could be no redemption glimpsed in the sudden configurations gathered among fragments. Redemption required complete commitment of one's contingent being, in the hope that faith could then deepen. Poetically that required using one's awareness of the limits of impersonality to ground a poetry so deeply personal that it could speak directly and seriously about its underlying belief structures. Therefore with the *Four Quartets* Eliot's impact no longer lay in any specific relational principles or fusions of the subjective and objective or exploration of distinctive imaginative sites. And this poetry did not bring stylistic imitations. Rather it had the more comprehensive effect of persuading poets like Jones and Spender and Tate and Lowell that Christianity could be a viable antidote to modernity's dissociated sensibility. In effect Eliot's struggle to be modern gave him the authority to define the limits of secular modernity and, more important, to use modernism's construction of ideal readers to define what Christianity might involve. The poet-maker had to give way to the listener, to one who can first hear what is contingent in voice and circumstance, and then bring to such hearing an intensity that attunes one to forces that extend beyond such contingency. Self-division in space and patience in time each opens us to an otherness paradoxically necessary for any satisfying view of individuality.

III

So far I have considered only general tendencies that Eliot established within modern poetry. An adequate analysis of his impact also requires studying how a range of poets use those examples, especially when that effort determines how they shape their stylistic options or change the overall ambitions of their work. However here I have only enough space to make some observations about three quite different concrete relations to Eliot—in the work of Hart Crane, John Ashbery, and Jorie Graham.

Crane's relationship to Eliot offers the purest example of impact one is likely to find. Discovering Eliot in 1918, as he was trying to understand how he could be a poet, he took Eliot as constituting what a modern poetry in English could be. This is the last stanza of Crane's "Black Tambourine" (1921):

> The black man, forlorn in the cellar,
> Wanders in some mid-kingdom, dark, that lies,
> Between his tambourine, stuck on the wall,
> And, in Africa, a carcass quick with flies.[12]

These are Eliot's quatrains; the voice has Eliot's strange distance that cannot quite escape identification; and, while not quite matching Eliot's "Sweeney Among the Nightingales," the poem has his distinctive stress on the image not for its perceptual qualities but for the way it projects a world suffused by feelings at once displacing and intensifying its objective properties. Here Crane seeks to capture within the object the intensity by which the subject comes to perceive his situation.

Even more Eliotic is the dialogue in the last stanzas of Crane's "Chaplinesque" between pitiless objectivity and the dream of locating an "infinitely gentle, infinitely suffering thing":

> And yet these fine collapses are not lies
> More than the pirouettes of any pliant cane:
> Our obsequies are, in a way, no enterprise.
> We can evade you, and all else but the heart:
> What blame to us if the heart live on.
>
> The game enforces smirks; but we have seen
> The moon in lonely alleys make
> A grail of laughter in an empty ash can,
> And through all sound of gaiety and quest
> Have heard a kitten in the wilderness.
>   (Crane, Weber [ed.] *Complete Poems*, p. 11)

Since Eliot was completing his *Waste Land* at the time Crane wrote this, he would not have been pleased by this kitten serving as the voice that sounds from the wilderness. Yet Crane almost gets away with such sentimentality because he bases his quest for a heart (and Hart) on his power to wield Eliotic fragments and Prufrockian phrases as instruments for finding within contemporary culture, rather than the past, a figure on whom to base his lyrical desires. Moreover his use of Eliot's blend of precision and strangeness proves the perfect lyric analogue for the intelligence that suffuses Chaplin's erratic pathos, as if Eliot gave Crane a way to locate a version of Whitman in Chaplin's too ample pockets, and thus to establish a mode of sympathy that the Eliotic aspects of the poem hold at an ironic distance.

Unfortunately this voice could not suffice. Having opened this space for sentiment or romance or shareable transformative sympathies, Crane had to give it features far more resonant than this kitten figure could provide. So he had to turn to his own version of *The Waste Land*'s mythic method, seeking what his "Marriage of Faustus and Helen" called an imagination that "spans beyond despair, / Outpacing bargain, vocable, and prayer" (Crane, Weber [ed.] *Complete poems*, p. 33). Responding to Eliot meant elaborating long poems on lyrical principles, and that meant seeking to build from allusions and the dense folding of distinctive levels of experience, ritual patterns which promised to release aspects of the secular world from their contingency, and hence from their pathos. One might even hope to make this very process of bridging the basis for a uniquely American vision outpacing Eliotic prayer.

However, a poetry so bound to Eliotic myth-constructing strategies may not be able to outpace prayer. Once one begins to seek underlying patterns as one's ground for values, the alternatives may remain religion, self-delusion, or despair. Or so at least it seems if we turn to the two contemporary poets I want to look at, each trying very different strategies for completing Crane's secular application of symbolist poetics to contemporary realities. For these poets, as for most contemporaries still in reaction to New Critical theologizings of Eliot's poetics, Eliot would matter not for his cult of pattern but for the opposite, for demonstrating a *via negativa* by which the most important psychic forces could work themselves free of interpretive practices developed to sustain the authority of empiricist analyses.

Take John Ashbery as our first example. When he mentions Eliot it is usually to establish distance between them, concealing how much they share (especially in the echoes of *Four Quartets* carried by the repetition of notions like "end" and "way" when Ashbery's "A Wave" meditates on love). Eliot becomes an emblem for the modernist anxieties that Ashbery hopes to transform. Thus he claims that Eliot is "wrong" in imagining hyacinths in bowls as somehow tragic: "life is life, no matter how artificial, how contrived the context." And, speaking of R. B. Kitaj's own use of Eliot, Ashbery remarks that Eliot seems to back away from his own discovery that the contiguity of fragments is "all their meaning," since meaning can only be understood as paralleling "the randomness and discontinuity of modern experience." Because "meaning cannot be truthfully defined as anything else," there simply is no escape from a horror of fragmentation and a sense of inescapable tragedy. There is only an openness to contradiction within and without, a "moving and not wanting to be moved, the loose / Meaning, untidy and simple like a threshing floor."[13]

And yet when we look at how Ashbery goes about developing lyrical values within these contradictions we find a remarkably positive embodiment of Eliotic stances. Ashbery's sense of fragments in social experience is complemented by a compelling concern for completeness in the rendering of the life of mind. As with Eliot, and with the best New Critical idealizations of Eliot, completeness is not a matter of attributing meanings to the world but of allowing the psyche to trace its own intricate turnings and doublings. This means refusing to bind oneself to the ego's demands for idealized images of itself. And it demands pushing poems to the point that they almost collapse under the burden of history embodied in the voices that play through it. But in encountering that limit Ashbery develops his own blend of Eliot's personal discursiveness in *Four Quartets* with the unceasing distanced self-consciousness of his earlier modes. The result is a strange quasi-discursiveness and disembodied, fleeting yet insistent personal presence that refuses any consolations by projected self-images. As Ashbery's discursiveness dissipates under the demands of the desire staging it, we find a commitment to capturing the full intricacy of consciousness inseparable from a Prufrockian dispersal of focus within the alternate meanings that metaphors introduce. However now the accepting of fragments allows even Prufrock to engage a "you," itself constantly shifting between referents as the modes of expression open different aspects of the speaking voice. For Ashbery can so transform Eliot that we realize the very notion of presence has much less to do with what one sees, or believes, than with how one manages to find release from the burden of trying to make the self more than the continual shifting of positions. Ultimately complexity of mind makes it possible to affirm an absolute simplicity for affective life—"ridiculous the waste sad time / stretching before and after."

Jorie Graham is more transcendentally inclined, echoing Eliot in part because she is adamant in refusing what she considers the banal secularity of the generation of (male) poets immediately preceding hers. Yet she refuses any thematic allegorizing or traditional spiritual foundations for that transcendence, contenting herself instead with the power to undo, and perhaps extend, our sense of sense by the force of her focused negative excess. The parallels to Eliot, and differences from her immediate predecessors, are most evident in two related domains— the sense of self she projects and the ways in which she uses cadence and gaps to sustain a personal pressure within fundamentally reflective, discursive meditations. Eve is Graham's model for personal agency because she finds her strength in her difference from Adam's righteousness, "liking that error, a feeling of being capable *in* an error."[14] It is only in this sense of one's own strangeness and contingency that one can locate a power not subsumed under some decorum or practice or demand from another. Then Graham employs this principle of error to open access to something beyond appearances. Here for example she identifies with Persephone returning to earth for the first time and imagining how the trees might reach beyond themselves to a perfection possible only if one can also identify with the unimaginable:

> that would bend more deeply into it inventing (if they could)
> another body, exploded, all leafiness, unimaginable
>
> by which to be forgiven by which to suffer completely this wind.

These are not Eliotic sentiments. But they depend for their force, as his *Four Quartets* do, on elaborate cadences and strategic silences as well as on a capacity to find plenitude within suffering which directly echoes Eliot's prayer to let his cry come unto God because he manages to identify with Mary's suffering. In fact one realizes through Graham how Eliot's rendering of gender is far more complex and open to internal multiplicity than are those we find in Yeats, Pound, and Williams. It ought to come as no surprise then that her most ambitious effort to locate herself within history is also her most overtly Eliotic poem. "Pollock and Canvas" equates the painter with the Fisher King, whose wound, and consequent refusal of mastery by the brush, becomes the only means of redeeming a land where the prevailing art kills what it tries to define. So she turns to Pollock for guidance in facing up to the contradictory pulls exerted by an ideal of the end of beauty: how can we at the end of one dream of beauty, repudiated completely in his destruction of illusionist space, still posit beauty as an end, and hence still desire the woman whom we know we can no longer contain within our paintings? There proves no answer, only the demand to let questions themselves carry a new definition of desire, cast out into an "open" free to take its own forms:

> Where does the end
>   begin?
> where does the lifting off of hands become
>   love,
> letting the made wade out into danger,
>   letting the form slur out into flaw, in
>
> conclusiveness? Where does the end of love
> begin? ...
>
> Where is the border of *stopping* and *ending*?
>   And the land was waste but the king did not die ...
> and the meaning of the rose rises up
>   (shedding the meaning of the rose)
> and the memory of the rose rises up
>   (shedding the memory of the rose)
>   (Jorie, *End of Beauty*, pp. 86–88)

IV

Close as Graham is to Eliot's *Quartets*, however, there remains an enormous distance between them—one which tells us almost as much about ourselves as it does about Eliot. For it leads us to the question of what in Eliot seems inimitable, and why. Crane provides a good beginning here because in so many respects he does capture Eliot's force. He embodies the anxiety over fragments and flat objectivity basic to Eliot, and he seeks the same abstract immediacy based on consciousness facing its own inescapable contradictions. But he does not linger on details enough to let them break through into obsessive states, nor does he let cadence and repetition and abstract pattern develop the full sense of invested intimacy that Eliot's characters come to bear. Similarly, Crane's kitten cannot wield the power of Eliot's "infinitely gentle, infinitely suffering thing," because Crane cannot muster the self-confidence, or self-torment, to generate so slow, so sensuous, so deliberate, and so painful a phrasing. And Crane must yield to an abstract hope that in Eliot is immediately countered by a defensive despair.

Ashbery affords a different set of contrasts. He is one of the few contemporaries to recover Eliot's versions of personal intimacy. Where most poets offer autobiographical melodrama, or flat narratives faintly hinting at deep dark personal tensions, or protracted engagements in the mysteries of memory, Ashbery maintains Eliot's blend of diffidence with a tremendous pressure of personal need within what seems discursive statement. Because of this sense of self, Ashbery is also brilliant at elaborating his own versions of Eliot's intricacy of self-consciousness, his internal play of metaphoric registers and tones, and (occasionally) his tortuous precision of diction. But no one among Eliot's heirs can muster the inhuman absoluteness of the "Son of man" passage in *The Waste Land* or the hallucinatory intensity of the concluding sections. And while a range of poets like Tate, Warren, Lowell, Jones, Heaney, and Crane could capture Eliot's sense of ghost-haunted history, no one but Eliot could combine that with the sense of immediate textures and tonal shifts that Ashbery manages to bring out as the other half of Eliot's projected incursiveness. Yet Ashbery can only be inclusive in his way by weakening the pressure of history and by treating heterogeneity as a matter of the psyche far more than as a matter of social forces. Some Ashbery, especially *Houseboat Days*, is obsessed by history, but only as a dump for metaphors and a reminder of poetic and personal belatedness. There is no sense of apocalypse or deep causal factors shaping psychic life— indeed Ashbery's strength is largely his insistence on weakening and relativizing history so that we are allowed neither nostalgia nor the modernists' idealized ambition.

Graham brings out contrasts that show off the accomplishments of Eliot's later poetry, largely by reminding us of how close the religious Eliot is to the kinds of values that women poets are now trying to foreground—for example in his refusing the traps posed by specular self-images, and in his abstract immediacy so intensely fusing subject and object that no clear distinction becomes possible. But her personal states make far more use of Eliot's gaps than they do of his ghosts, since history enters her work only in highly abstract ways. Similarly, she must provide a dynamic syntax expressing her personal presence primarily by imposing an ecstatic mode, as if the sources of eloquence were always hovering behind the language without quite growing out of the specific linguistic structure. Compare the repetitious features of Graham's cadences with Eliot's amazing pull between the insistence of rhythm and the fluidity of syntax:

> Time present and time past
> Are both perhaps present in time future,
> And time future contained in time past ...
> What might have been is an abstraction
> Remaining a perpetual possibility
> Only in a world of speculation.
> What might have been and what has been
> Point to one end, which is always present.   (*BN* 1)

Finally, the contrast with Graham invites an Eliotic irony: perhaps the strength of his syntax derives in large part from the fact that Eliot need not make the presence of ecstatic states the measure of the poem's possible significance. He can be content with using poetry as testimony for ideals and principles that lie beyond poetry, informing it and given historicity through it. Graham, on the other hand, wants a transcendental register without being able to trust any ideas about that transcendence (although her more recent book *Region of Unlikeness* sounds much of contemporary thought in quest of those ideas). Therefore she cannot just testify to the power of certain principles—her poems must constitute both the idea and its efficacy, and hence they are haunted by a pressure to make gestures of breathless excitement bear much of the burden in giving content to what cannot actually be said. The more ridiculous appears the sad waste time stretching before and after, the more desperate poetry may become to do more than perhaps anyone can with the present.

NOTES

1. I see this essay as an opportunity to ally from a different perspective with those now attempting to show how thin this dominant negative account is and how much we lose if remain content with it. The critics whom I think provide the best lines for such a recovery are Michael Levenson, Ronald Bush, and, for the contemporary currency of Eliot's ideas, Richard Shusterman. Also important from a different perspective is Gregory Jay's demonstration of how much of Eliot can fit into poststructuralist studies.

2. Williams, *Autobiography*, p. 174. The quotation above is from Williams, *Selected Essays*, pp. 22–23.

3. Yeats's critique is most emphatic in his "Modern Poetry." The view of Auden derives from Edward Mendelson, *Early Auden*, pp. xx; 28–31, 13rff. For Shapiro see his *Defense of Ignorance*. The two anthologies I refer to are Hall, *Contemporary American Poetry*, and Allen, *New American Poetry*, and similar claims are made by Poulin, *Contemporary American Poetry*. Kenner's view are outlined in his *Pound Era*, and explicitly argued in "The Possum in the Cave." Perloff makes her basic argument in *Poetics of Indeterminacy*, then uses Eliot as a figure of closure to contract with a more capacious postmodern openness to the world in her *Poetic License*.

4. Orwell is quoted in a very useful book for my purposes, Raffel (ed.) *Possum*, p. 35.

5. Hart Crane, letters to Alan Tate and to Gorham Munson, January 1923, in Weber (ed.) *Letters*, pp. 114–15.

6. Bogan in Raffel (ed.), *Possum*, p. 37.

7. Raffel (ed.), *Possum*, p. 38.

8. I echo in my description passages from Eliot's account of impersonality in "Tradition and the Individual Talent," in his *SE* (1950), pp. 7, 9–11.

9. Mendelson, *Early Auden*, pp. 28–29.

10. Virginia Woolf, "A Room of One's Own," as cited by Amy Clampitt, "Prefaces."

11. David Antin elaborates this point in his "Modernism and Postmodernism."

12. Weber (ed.) *Complete Poems*, p. 4.

13. I refer to essays on Nell Blaine and Kitaj in Ashbery's *Reported Sightings*, pp. 237–37, 301–2, 306–8j; and for the poetry, to Ashbery's *Selected Poems*, p. 88.

14. Jorie Graham, *End of Beauty*, p. 7. The passage below is from p. 63.

Works Cited

Allen, Donald, (ed.). *The New American Poetry, 1945–1960*. New York: Grove Press, 1960.

Anrin, David. "Modernism and Postmodernism: Approaching the Present in American Poetry," *Boundary* 2, 1.1 (1972).

Ashbery, John. *Reported Sightings: Art Chronicles, 1957–87*, David Bergman (ed.). Cambridge, MA: MIT Press, 1991.

Bush, Ronald. "T. S. Eliot and Modernism at the Present Time: A Provocation," Bush, ed. *T. S. Eliot: The Modernist in History*. Cambridge: Cambridge University Press, 1991, pp. 191–204.

Camplitt, Amy. "Prefaces: Five Poets on Poems by T. S. Eliot," *Yale Review* 78.2 (1989): 196–99.

Crane, Hart. *The Complete Poems, and Selected Letters and Prose*, Brom Weber, (ed.). Garden City: Anchor, 1966.

———. *Letters of Hart Crane*, Brom Weber (ed.). Los Angeles: University of California Press, 1965.

Graham, Jorie. *The End of Beauty*. New York: Ecco Press, 1987.

Hall, Donald, (ed.). *Contemporary American Poetry*. Baltimore: Penguin, 1963.

Jay, Gregory. *T. S. Eliot and the Poetics of Literary History*. Baton Rouge: Louisiana State University Press, 1983.

Kenner, Hugh. *The Pound Era*. Berkeley: University of California Press, 1971.

———. "The Possum in the Cave," Stephen J. Greenblatt (ed.). *Allegory and Representation*. Baltimore: John Hopkins Pres, 1981, pp. 120–44.

Mendelson, Edward. *Early Auden*. New York: Viking Press, 1981.

Perloff, Marjorie. *The Poetics of Indeterminacy: Rimbaud to Cage*. Princeton: Princeton University Press, 1981.

———. *Poetic License*. Evanston: Northwestern University Press, 1990.

Poulin, A. Jr. (ed.). *Contemporary American Poetry*. Boston: Houghton Mifflin, 1st edn., 1968.

Raffel, Burton (ed.). *Possum and Old Ez in the Public Eye*. Boston: Archon Books, 1985.

Shapiro, Karl. *Defense of Ignorance*. New York: Random House, 1960.

Shusterman, Richard. *T. S. Eliot and the Philosophy of Criticism*. New York: Columbia University Press, 1988.

Williams, William Carlos. *Autobiography*. New York: New Directions, 1967.

———. *Selected Essays of William Carlos Williams*. New York: Random House, 1954.

Woolf, Virginia. *A Room of One's Own*. New York: Harcourt, Brace, Jovanovich, 1957.

Yeats, William Butler. "Modern Poetry," (1938) in his *Essays and Introductions* (London: Macmillan, 1961).

Chronology

1888	Thomas Stearns Eliot is born September 26, in St. Louis.
1906–10	Eliot is an undergraduate at Harvard.
1910–11	Studies in Paris. Writes "Preludes," "Prufrock," "Portrait of a Lady," "Rhapsody on a Windy Night," and "La Figlia che Piange."
1911–14	Eliot is a graduate student in philosophy at Harvard. Begins dissertation on the philosophy of F. H. Bradley.
1914	Travels to England; meets the poet Ezra Pound.
1915–16	"Prufrock" is published; Eliot teaches in London; completes thesis on Bradley; marries Vivienne Haigh-Wood.
1917–19	Works at Lloyd's Bank; *Prufrock and Other Observations* published.
1920	*Poems* and *The Sacred Wood* are published. Eliot begins *The Waste Land*.
1922	Eliot is editor of *The Criterion*; wins Dial Award for *The Waste Land*.
1925	*The Hollow Men* and *Poems, 1909–25* are published. Eliot leaves the banks and goes to work for the publisher Faber & Gwyer.
1927	Becomes a member of the Church of England and a British citizen. Begins writing the *Ariel Poems*.
1928	*For Lancelot Andrewes* is published.
1930	*Ash Wednesday* is published.

1931	*Coriolan* and *Thoughts After Lambeth* are published.
1932–33	Visits the United States for the first time since 1914; lectures at Harvard; visits Emily Hale in California; separates permanently from his first wife.
1934	*The Rock* is published.
1935–36	Writes *Murder in the Cathedral* and *Collected Poems, 1909–35,* including "Burnt Norton."
1939	*The Idea of a Christian Society,* a series of lectures Eliot gave at Cambridge, is published, as is *The Family Reunion.*
1940–44	Writes the *Four Quartets.*
1945	Shares an apartment with John Hayward until 1957.
1947	Eliot's first wife Vivienne dies.
1948	Eliot is awarded the Nobel Prize for Literature; writes *Notes Toward a Definition of Culture.*
1950	Writes *The Cocktail Party.*
1951	Begins to have health problems related to his heart.
1957	Marries Valerie Fletcher.
1962–63	Becomes seriously ill after a period of smog in London.
1965	Dies in London on January 4.

Works by T.S. Eliot

POETRY

Prufrock and Other Observations (1917)
Poems (1919)
Ara Vos Prec (1920)
Poems (1920)
The Waste Land (1922)
Poems, 1909–1925 (1925)
Journey of the Magi (1927)
A Song for Simeon (1928)
Animula (1929)
Ash Wednesday (1930)
Marina (1930)
Triumphal March (1931)
Collected Poems, 1909–1935 (1936)
Old Possum's Book of Practical Cats (1939)
East Coker (1940)
Burnt Norton (1941)
The Dry Salvages (1941)
Little Gidding (1942)
Four Quartets (1944)
The Complete Poems and Plays, 1909–1950 (1952)
Collected Poems, 1909–1962 (1963)

Poems Written in Early Youth (1967)

The Complete Pomes and Plays of T.S. Eliot (1969)

Inventions of the March Hare: Poems 1909–1917, ed. Christopher Ricks
    (1996)

DRAMA

Sweeney Agonistes (1932)

The Rock (1934)

Murder in the Cathedral (1935)

The Family Reunion (1939)

The Cocktail Party (1950)

The Confidential Clerk (1954)

The Elder Statesman (1959)

Collected Plays (1962)

PROSE

Ezra Pound, His Metric and His Poetry (1918)

The Sacred Wood (1920)

Andrew Marvell (1922)

Homage to John Dryden (1924)

For Lancelot Andrewes (1928)

Dante (1929)

Tradition and Experimentation in Present-Day Literature (1929)

Thoughts After Lambeth (1931)

Selected Essays 1917–1932 (1932)

John Dryden: The Poet, the Dramatist, the Critic (1932)

The Use of Poetry and the Use of Criticism (1933)

After Strange Gods (1934)

Elizabethan Essays (1934)

Essays Ancient and Modern (1936)

The Idea of a Christian Society (1939)

The Classics and The Man of Letters (1942)
Notes Towards the Definition of Culture (1948)
Poetry and Drama (1951)
The Three Voices of Poetry (1954)
Religious Drama: Mediaeval and Modern (1954)
On Poetry and Poets (1957)
George Herbert (1962)
Knowledge and Experience in the Philosophy of F.H. Bradley (1964)
To Criticize the Critic, and other Writings (1965)
Selected Prose of T.S. Eliot, ed. Frank Kermode (1975)

Works about T.S. Eliot

Ackroyd, Peter. *T.S. Eliot: A Life*. New York: Simon and Schuster, 1984.

Allan, Mowbray. *T.S. Eliot's Impersonal Theory of Poetry*. Lewisburg, PA: Bucknell University Press, 1974.

Antrim, Harry T. *T.S. Eliot's Concept of Language*. Gainsville, FL: University of Florida Humanities Monographs, 1971.

Asher, Kenneth. *T.S. Eliot and Ideology*. London: Cambridge University Press, 1997.

Basu, Tapan Kumar, ed. *T.S. Eliot: An Anthology of Recent Criticism*. Delhi: Pencraft International, 1933.

Bedient, Calvin. *He Do the Police in Different Voices:* The Waste Land *and its Protagonist*. Chicago: University of Chicago Press, 1986.

Beehler, Michael. *T.S. Eliot, Wallace Stevens, and the Discourses of Difference*. Baton Rouge: Louisiana State University Press, 1987.

Bergonzi, Bernard. *T.S. Eliot*. New York: Macmillan, 1972.

Bloom, Harold, ed. *T.S. Eliot's* The Waste Land. New York: Chelsea House, 1986.

Bolgan, Anne C. *What the Thunder Really Said: A Retrospective Essay on the Making of* The Waste Land. Montreal: McGill-Queen's University Press, 1973.

Brooker, Jewel Spears. *Mystery and Escape: T.S. Eliot and the Dialectic of Modernism*. Boston: University of Massachusetts Press, 1996.

Bush, Ronald. *T.S. Eliot: A Study in Character and Style*. New York: Oxford University Press, 1983.

Christ, Carol T. "T.S. Eliot and the Victorians." *Modern Philology* (November 1981).

Clarke, Graham, ed. *T.S. Eliot: Critical Assessments*. London: Christopher Helm, 1990. 4 vols.

Cook, Eleanor. "T.S. Eliot and the Carthaginian Peace." *ELH* 46 (1979): 341–45.

Cookson, Linda and Bryan Loughrey, eds. *Critical Essays on* The Waste Land. Harlow: Longmans, 1988.

Cooper, John Xiros. *T.S. Eliot and the* Four Quartets. London: Cambridge, 1996.

Cuddy, Lois A. *T.S. Eliot and the Poetics of Evolution.* Lewisburg, Penn.: Bucknell University Press, 2000.

Davidson, Harriet. *T.S. Eliot.* New York: Longman, 1999.

Donker, Marjorie. "*The Waste Land* and the *Aeneid.*" *PMLA* 89 (1974): 164–71.

Donoghue, Denis. *Words Alone.* New Haven, Conn.: Yale University Press, 2000.

Eliot, Valerie, ed. The Waste Land: *A Facsimile and Transcript of the Original Drafts, Including the Annotations of Ezra Pound.* New York: Harcourt Brace Jovanovich, 1971.

Everett, Barbara. "Eliot's Marianne: *The Waste Land* and Its Poetry of Europe." *The Review of English Studies* 31, no. 121 (1980): 41–53.

Frye, Northrup. *T.S. Eliot.* New York: Capricorn Books, 1963.

Gallup, Donald. *T.S. Eliot: A Bibliography.* Rev. Ed. New York: Harcourt Brace Jovanovich, 1969.

Gardner, Helen. *The Art of T.S. Eliot.* New York: Dutton, 1950.

Gish, Nancy K. The Waste Land: *A Poem of Memory and Desire.* Boston: Twayne, 1988.

Gordon, Lyndall. *An Imperfect Life.* New York: Norton, 2000.

Grant, Michael, ed. *T.S. Eliot: The Critical Heritage.* 2 vols. London: Routledge & Kegan Paul, 1982.

Hough, Graham. *Reflections on a Literary Revolution.* Washington, D.C.: The Catholic University of America Press, 1960.

Jay, Gregory. *T.S. Eliot and the Poetics of Literary History.* Baton Rouge: Louisiana State University Press, 1983.

Julius, Anthony. *T.S. Eliot: Anti-Semitism and Literary Form.* London: Cambridge, 1996.

Kim, Dal-Yong. *Puritan Sensibility in T.S. Eliot's Poetry.* New York: Peter Lang, 1994.

Litz, A. Walton, ed. *Eliot in His Time: Essays on the Occasion of the Fiftieth Anniversary of* The Waste Land. Princeton: Princeton University Press, 1973.

Kenner, Hugh. *The Invisible Poet: T.S. Eliot*. London: W.H. Allen, 1960.

————, ed. *T.S. Eliot: A Collection of Critical Essays*. Englewood Cliffs, NJ: Prentice-Hall, 1965.

Kojecky, Roger. *T.S. Eliot's Social Criticism*. New York: Farrar, Straus and Giroux, 1971.

Malamud, Randy. *T.S. Eliot's Drama*. Westport, Conn.: Greenwood, 1992.

Manganiello, Dominic. *T.S. Eliot and Dante*. New York: St. Martin's Press, 1989.

Moody, David A. *The Cambridge Companion to T.S. Eliot*. London: Cambridge, 1994.

North, Michael. *The Political Aesthetic of Yeats, Eliot, and Pound*. Cambridge: Cambridge University Press, 1991.

Olney, James, ed. *T.S. Eliot: Essays from the Southern Review*. Oxford: Oxford University Press, 1988.

Oser, Lee. *T.S. Eliot and American Poetry*. New York: Cahners, 1998.

Phillips, Caroline. *Religious Quest in the Poetry of T.S. Eliot*. Lewiston: Edwin Mellen, 1995.

Pinkney, Toney. *Women in the Poetry of T.S. Eliot: A Psychoanalytic Approach*. London: Macmillan, 1984.

Ricks, Christopher. *T.S. Eliot and Prejudice*. London: Faber and Faber, 1988.

Schuchard, Ronald. *Eliot's Dark Angel*. London: Oxford University Press, 1999.

Shusterman, Richard M. *T.S. Eliot and the Philosophy of Criticism*. New York: Universe, 1999.

Sigg, Eric. *The American T.S. Eliot*. London: Cambridge, 1990.

Smith, Grover Cleveland. *T.S. Eliot and the Use of Memory*. Lewisburg, Penn.: Bucknell University Press, 1996.

————. *T.S. Eliot's Poetry and Plays: A Study in Sources and Meaning*. Chicago: The University of Chicago Press, 1956.

Southam, B.C. *A Student's Guide to the Selected Poems of T.S. Eliot*. Boston: Faber and Faber, 1990.

Spurr, David. *Conflicts in Consciousness: T.S. Eliot's Poetry and Criticism*. Champaign, Ill.: University of Illinois Press, 1990.

Surette, Leon. *The Birth of Modernism: Ezra Pound, T.S. Eliot, W. B. Yeats, and the Occult*. New York: McGill University Press, 1994.

Svarny, Eric. *The Men of 1914: T.S. Eliot and Early Modernism.* New York: Open University Press, 1990.

Tamplin, Ronald. *A Preface to T.S. Eliot.* New York: Longman, 1987.

Tate, Allen, ed. *T.S. Eliot: The Man and His Work.* New York: Delacorte Press, 1966.

Unger, Leonard. *T.S. Eliot: Moment and Patterns.* Minneapolis: University of Minnesota Press, 1961.

———, ed. *T.S. Eliot: A Selected Critique.* New York: Russell & Russell, 1966.

Ward, David. *T.S. Eliot Between Two Worlds: A Reading of T.S. Eliot's Poetry and Plays.* Boston: Routledge & Kegan Paul, 1973.

Williams, Geoffrey B. *A Reason in a Storm.* New York: University Press of America, 1991.

Williamson, George. *A Reader's Guide to T.S. Eliot: A Poem-by-Poem Analysis.* New York: Farrar, Straus & Giroux, 1966.

Xiros, John. *T.S. Eliot's Orchestra.* New York: Garland, 2000.

WEBSITES

Exploring *The Waste Land*
world.std.com/~raparker/exploring/thewasteland/explore.html

T.S. Eliot—The Academy of American Poets
www.poets.org/academy/news/tseli

The T.S. Eliot Page
www.english.uga.edu/~232/eliot.taken.html

The T.S. Eliot Society
www.arts.ualberta.ca/~eliotsoc/

T.S. Eliot Reads *The Waste Land*
town.hall.org/Archives/radio/IMS/HarperAudio/011894_harp_ITH.html

TSE: The Web Site
www.missouri.edu/~tselist/tse.html

What the Thunder Said: T.S. Eliot
www.deathclock.com/thunder/index.html

Contributors

HAROLD BLOOM is Sterling Professor of the Humanities at Yale University and Henry W. and Albert A. Berg Professor of English at the New York University Graduate School. He is the author of over 20 books, including *Shelley's Mythmaking* (1959), *The Visionary Company* (1961), *Blake's Apocalypse* (1963), *Yeats* (1970), *A Map of Misreading* (1975), *Kabbalah and Criticism* (1975), *Agon: Toward a Theory of Revisionism* (1982), *The American Religion* (1992), *The Western Canon* (1994), and *Omens of Millennium: The Gnosis of Angels, Dreams, and Resurrection* (1996). *The Anxiety of Influence* (1973) sets forth Professor Bloom's provocative theory of the literary relationships between the great writers and their predecessors. His most recent books include *Shakespeare: The Invention of the Human* (1998), a 1998 National Book Award finalist, *How to Read and Why* (2000), and *Genius: A Mosaic of One Hundred Exemplary Creative Minds* (2002). In 1999, Professor Bloom received the prestigious American Academy of Arts and Letters Gold Medal for Criticism, and in 2002 he received the Catalonia International Prize.

ELLYN SANNA has authored more than 50 books, including adult nonfiction, novels, young adult biographies, and gift books. She also works as a freelance editor and manages an editorial service.

PORTIA WILLIAMS WEISKEL has taught English and journalism in both high school and adult education atmospheres, and has done freelance copyediting for numerous colleges. Her publications include writings on Joyce, Tolstoy, and Wilder.

F.O. MATTHIESSEN was Professor of English and History at Harvard from 1929–1950. His books include *American Renaissance* (1941), *Henry James: The Major Phase* (1944), and *The Acheivement of T.S. Eliot* (1947).

CLEANTH BROOKS was a leading New Critic of the 1940s–1950s and Professor of English at Yale between 1946–1975. He is recognized for his critical acuity in close readings of modern literature in *The Well Wrought Urn* (1947) and other essays. He has published important works on Milton, Thomas Percy and William Faulkner.

CHARLES ALTIERI is Professor of English at Berkeley with a specialty in twentieth-century poetry and the visual arts. His books include *Painterly Abstraction in Modernist American Poetry: The Contemporaneity of Modernism* (1989) and *Postmodernisms Now* (1998).

INDEX